So you think you .

That black-and-white picture in your mind may need a little fine-tuning. With this book, Eddie Chu takes you on a biblical journey of discovery. You will see there is more than one way to view your heavenly Father and His interactions with you and the world. Perhaps the Holy Spirit wants to add a bit more color to your perception of the Father and His redemptive purpose in Christ. Expect to be challenged. Expect to be changed.

—David Kitz,
award-winning author of *The Soldier, The Terrorist,
and the Donkey King.*

All of us approach issues surrounding God, justice, punishment, and grace with some unquestioned assumptions. Many struggle to build a coherent understanding of God as our Father who describes His throne as a mercy seat. Every thoughtful Christian will find thought-provoking insights into issues that demand attention in *Seeing God Differently.*

—Malcolm Seath,
Pharmaceutical CEO and Church Leader

How *do* you reconcile the character of God as a disciplined Judge who would send people to Hell, and God as a loving Father full of compassion and forgiveness? Eddie Chu dares to tackle this dilemma with courage and meticulous research, and what has come forth is a book that every pastor, every theologian, and indeed every Christian should have on their bookshelf… but not to gather dust; you've got to read it and live by it!

Eddie writes from personal experiences that forced him to take another look at something we have all probably taken for granted. It will revolutionize your thinking and revolutionize your effectiveness as an evangelical Christian. Be prepared to have your traditional perspectives challenged, but also be prepared to have your love for God deepened and enriched.

Thank you, Eddie, for writing this book.

—Terry Bridle,
thirty-year missionary to Eastern Europe,
Christian Radio Producer

SEEING
GOD
DIFFERENTLY

a fresh look at
OUR UNCHANGING FATHER

Eddie Chu

SEEING GOD DIFFERENTLY

Printed in Canada

ISBN: 978-1-77069-740-9

Word Alive Press
131 Cordite Road, Winnipeg, MB R3W 1S1
www.wordalivepress.ca

Cataloguing in Publication may be obtained through Library and Archives Canada.

ABOUT THE BOOK

Prominent doctrines of the Bible often don't agree, so what makes a certain interpretation of the Bible seem right or wrong? The perceived rightness or wrongness of a doctrine depends on whether it fits within a framework of mutually supportive doctrines. When an alternative doctrine doesn't fit within that framework, the defenders of the framework discredit it.

One such alternative doctrine goes like this: God may not be the immovable judge the church has made Him out to be. But suggest this to most Christians and you'll be faced with a number of tricky "What about...?" questions that require careful thought and consideration. One by one, *Seeing God Differently* answers these questions, helping you gain fresh insight into the powerful parental love of God.

ABOUT THE AUTHOR

Eddie grew up in Hong Kong under a mixture of eastern and western religious influences. Becoming a Christian in Toronto in 1978, he later completed the core requirements of the Master of Theological Studies degree at Tyndale University College and Seminary. He and his wife Kathy have been married for thirty-eight years and have two children, Jason and Irene. Eddie and Kathy now make their home in Ottawa.

Contents

 # Acknowledgements

During the last three decades, many Christian writers have influenced my knowledge of God and the Bible. In particular the following authors, in alphabetical order, have contributed to my understanding of God as Father. To them I express my thanks.

Tony Campolo, well known for his compassionate service to the poor and marginalized, taught me about faith in action for compassion and justice. In his books and downloaded sermons, through his deeds, humor, and insight, Tony showed me the Father's love in motion.

Oswald Chambers, author of the best-selling devotional *My Utmost for His Highest*, has shaped and deepened my faith in God through my numerous early-morning *Aha!* moments. His uncanny insight into the heart and mind of God has been invaluable throughout my spiritual journey.

C. Baxter Kruger introduced me to the Trinity like no other author has. His teaching about the perfect circle of inclusive love of God helped me understand and experience to new depths the exciting and unfathomable love of the Father.

Christopher Marshall, author of *Compassionate Justice* and *Beyond Retribution* and a leading writer and expert on Biblical justice, opened my eyes to restorative justice and provided the most pivotal insight into understanding what it means when God administers justice. The chapter about biblical justice is mostly based on what I learned from reading Chris' books and speaking with him.

Brian McLaren is the author of many books but the one that got me started was *A New Kind of Christian*. Brian yanked me out of the exclusivism paradigm and introduced me to a gentler and kinder God. Over the years, I have followed most of Brian's books, much to my liberation from an exclusive and judgmental spiritual upbringing.

Philip Yancey's *Fearfully and Wonderfully Made,* coauthored with Paul Brand, has gotten me hooked on Yancey for the last few decades, and the rest is history. His view on Christ in *What's So Amazing About Grace* and *The Jesus I Never Knew,* in particular, revealed the biblical Jesus Christ to me as no other writer could.

As I survey my bookshelves, there are really too many books to list. The writers I mentioned have taught me the most and have shaped the theological framework that helped me answer the many "What about…?" questions that bugged me for decades.

Evan Braun from Word Alive Press deserves a big thank you. His constructive criticism and encouragement have helped shape this book.

Finally, the one person who has taught me the most about parental love is Kathy, my wife, lover, and friend for almost forty years. Her unconditional love and care for our son and daughter, Jason and Irene, and just about anyone who crosses her path, has taught me more about God's parental love than any other human I have met.

Introduction

Come on out come on out
Into the light
There is no jury
There is no judge
Ready and waiting
Are the steady arms of love[1]

The most common title for God in the Bible is Father. If you search the most popular versions of the New Testament, you'll find that the word *Father* occurs nearly 230 times. In contrast, God is called Judge just five times, once in Acts and four times in the Epistles, and *never* by Jesus in the Gospels. Most evangelicals, however, believe God is a judge who *must* punish all sinners with the penalty of eternal separation from God so as to maintain and uphold God's holiness, righteousness, and justice.

Although this term establishes one explanation of the death of Christ on the cross, it forces people to view God *first* as an immovable judge administering inflexible justice. Only after receiving the judge's pardon through Christ can anyone experience God as a loving parent reconciling humankind through amazing grace in Jesus Christ. The mission of this book is to provide an alternative that causes us to relate to God *first* as Father.

When I tried to share this idea with other Christians—that it isn't necessary to view God as a judge who imposes on all humankind the penalty of eternal separation—most evangelicals asked a "What about…?" question. After I answered one, another would pop up. This went on and on, resulting in inconclusive dialogues.

This is because of a doctrinal framework that builds its foundation on a judge-first view of God. Most people assume that the judge-first view is the only credible explanation of Christ's sacrifice. Many I've spoken with, including seasoned pastors, don't even know there are biblically sound alternatives.

The judge-first view of God explains, to some extent, why Christians—and evangelicals in particular—are viewed by western society as judgmental and intolerant. Believing that God is predominantly a judge forces us to accept that we deserve God's judgment and punishment before we can accept God's forgiveness through Christ. The "What about… ?" questions are based on a coherent framework of judge-first interpretations of certain Bible passages.

In my quest to seek the basis of these questions, I discovered there were biblically sound parent-first interpretations. Through my seeking answers to my evangelical friends' "What about…?" questions, a fresh parent-first view of God emerged. The view is based on a biblically coherent framework and helped me arrive at an alternative answer to a question many thoughtful Christians often ask: Why did Jesus have to die on the Cross to reconcile sinners to God?[2]

The traditional explanation of Jesus' sacrifice forces us to consider God first as a judge who finds it necessary to punish all sinners. If I want to convince my unchurched friends that they need Jesus in their lives, I have to first prove that they're worthy of eternal damnation. Often, they feel that Christians like me are judging them.

If we are able to consider God first as a loving parent and still come to a biblically sound understanding of why Christ died on the cross, we might interact with others differently. We might be able to demonstrate the love of Christ without first insisting that people accept the necessity of a punishing God.

In sharing with my evangelical friends, I found that very few were open to interpretations opposed to their traditional understanding. The more thoughtful took time to listen and usually came into agreement, eventually adopting the parent-first attitude, provided we had enough interactions to tackle several of the "What about... ?" questions.

These interactions motivated me to write this, my first book. The only way to convince those who are willing to listen is to show that there are biblically sound parent-first alternative answers to the questions.

As I tackled these questions over time, a parent-first framework emerged. Since the alternative answers to the "What about... ?" questions are biblically sound, the emerging framework is biblically coherent. Eventually, after numerous discussions with thoughtful Christian friends, open-minded Bible teachers, and supportive seminary professors, I found an explanation for the sacrifice of Christ that doesn't require us to first take the view that God must punish all sinners with eternal death.

Some readers, and evangelicals in particular, may be ready to throw this book down. I don't blame you. It was difficult for me, too, to consider other explanations. For thoughtful Christians who aren't afraid to explore biblical alternatives, however, I urge to you try a few "What about... ?" questions and see if the answers have sound biblical support.

Each "What about... ?" question represents a fork in the road—a choice—to understanding the parental heart of God as an alternative to the immovable Judge. As we consistently explore the choices that lead to a parental heart, we arrive at an unfamiliar but delightful destination: the heart of God as our loving Father.

I invite you to take this journey with me. At first, it will be uncomfortable but I urge you to keep several versions of the Bible handy—along with Greek and Hebrew dictionaries, if you have them—study the Bible passages with care, and consider the alternatives.

What About Those Who Have Never Heard?

ONE

QUESTIONING A BASIC DOCTRINE

"Sometimes the tension within me was so intense that I thought I was going to explode," Scott said to me over lunch one day.

Scott was the youth pastor at our church in Toronto some years back. He has since moved on to running a small technology company we started more than ten years ago. We remained good friends over the years and kept in touch.

He and his wife stopped attending church. Many acquaintances interpreted this to mean that he'd abandoned his faith. When we got together, we got into intense discussions about Christianity and church. During these discussions, it was clear to me that Scott hadn't abandoned his faith but was questioning certain popular evangelical doctrines.

As our youth pastor in the mid-1990s, Scott ran a successful children's and youth ministry. Under his direction our little church attracted children and youth from the neighborhood in numbers beyond what our congregation size would normally justify. He was committed to his ministry and enthusiastic about reaching out to children and youth with the love of Jesus Christ. One year, through Kidz Camp, our summer program, more than forty children were "born again." In other words, they prayed to accept Christ as their Lord and Savior.

For those who are unfamiliar with the typical evangelical doctrine about salvation, I think this requires some explanation.

The doctrine of evangelical churches like ours teaches that unless someone is born again by accepting Jesus Christ as Lord and Savior, usually through a sincere "sinner's prayer", that person will go to hell at the end of his or her earthly life. Hell means different things to different people, but most agree it's a place of intense suffering without the presence of God. It's a terrible place with a one-way door; after people get into hell, they're stuck there for all eternity and there's no way out. Further, there is no second chance beyond this life. Since God's will is that none should perish, most evangelicals believe that God's calling for us is to help as many as possible become born-again Christians.

Our doctrine further explains why everyone should become Christian. It goes somewhat like this: God is righteous, just, and holy. Since God is righteous, he requires righteousness in humankind, and most interpret *righteousness* as a state of total purity untainted by sin. Since God is just, he cannot leave sins unpunished. Most evangelicals adhere to a doctrine that teaches that God must punish each and every sin in each and every human being. If God were to leave any sin or sinner unpunished, God would be offending His own attribute of justice. A perfect God cannot, and will not, allow His perfect attributes to be offended or violated. Therefore, by virtue of His perfection, God must punish sinners with eternal separation from Him.

Since God is holy, he cannot establish a loving relationship with anyone who's contaminated by sin. The Bible teaches that "all have sinned and fall short of the glory of God" (Romans 3:23, NIV), which means every human being is a sinner and falls short of God's requirement for righteousness. Since the wages of sin is death (Romans 6:23), all sinners must suffer the consequence of sin, which is eternal separation from God. Sinners cannot enter the presence of a holy God and have a loving relationship with Him unless something is done to remove, pay for, or atone for their sins.

On the other hand, the Bible teaches that God wants no one to perish (2 Peter 3:9). This would lead some to explain, "To a certain extent, God has a problem." God is love. God loves each and every one of us, and God loves perfectly. But we are sinners—each and every one of us—and sin must be punished. God doesn't want to see any of us suffer the punishment of sin, to be separated from His love and suffer in hell. Therefore, to reconcile this "problem," God became human through Jesus Christ, lived a sinless life,[3] and offered Himself to take the punishment of our sins. In more theological terms, God incarnated as perfect and sinless Jesus Christ, then offered Himself as the atonement (at-one-ment) for our sins to take the punishment that's intended for us sinners. God the Father accepts the atonement of God the Son as substitution for our penalty to meet His requirement for justice and righteousness, thus balancing the divine scales of justice.

Those who admit they're sinners and receive the atonement of Christ by faith as a gift in substitution for the penalty they deserve, receive God's forgiveness as though they hadn't sinned at all. They are "justified" through faith in Christ. Most evangelicals accept this as the only explanation for Jesus' sacrifice.

Forgiveness through the atonement of Christ, like any gift, must be accepted by the receiver. The sinner's prayer is a way to express one's desire to receive God's forgiveness, become a Christian, and avoid the horrible fate of entering hell. This prayer has countless variations, but generally it goes like this:

> Dear God, I admit that I'm a sinner. As a result, I deserve eternal condemnation and separation from You. I'm thankful that Jesus Christ has come to live and die, taking my penalty on my behalf. I am sorry for my sins. I now surrender control of my life to Jesus Christ. Since Jesus Christ has taken my penalty, I'm now acceptable to you and can enjoy your love and presence now and forever. Thank you and amen.

Those who don't have the opportunity to receive this gift or have had opportunities but refuse it, remain guilty and unforgiven by God.

3

As a result, upon the end of this life, they face the wrath of God and receive the penalty of sin—death and separation from God in hell.

Or at least so says the judge-first explanation.

NEIGHBORHOOD KIDS

Our church's neighborhood was highly multicultural. There were people from all over the world, including China, Sri Lanka, Pakistan, India, Eastern Europe, Russia, the West Indies, and the Middle East. Most important for our church was to make sure other people go to heaven by being born again, and we're born again when we sincerely pray some form of the sinner's prayer. Therefore, it was important that the children who went to our church camp have the opportunity to become Christians.

Kids had fun at the camp. In addition to games and crafts, they had Bible learning programs specifically designed to include games, songs, and stories that explained the love of God as expressed through Jesus Christ. They received genuine love and care from the program workers. Typically, a program would wrap up with an invitation for the children to invite Jesus into their hearts so they could be born again.

> *Never mind that the program grew from a few dozen children to more than a hundred, if there were no head count of the children "coming to the Lord," what was the point?*

The purpose of our camp wasn't just to give the children something meaningful and fun to do during summer vacation, keeping them off the streets and out of their parents' hair; we wanted to expose them to Christianity. Although a biblical and worthwhile goal, some people at the church wondered aloud whether the program could be considered effective if the camp organizers didn't provide statistics proving how many children "came to the Lord" by inviting Jesus Christ into their hearts as Savior. Never mind that the program grew from a few dozen children to more than a hundred; if there was no head count of the children "coming to the Lord," what was the point?[4]

It didn't take Scott long to notice that there was something wrong with that attitude. These children came from all over the world. Their families had different religious and cultural backgrounds. Depending on their backgrounds, the children had varying degrees of receptivity to Christianity. After having fun and enjoying the affection of the program workers, the kids tended to be very receptive to invitations from such trusted sources as the camp counselors. When the counselors told them about God's love and how they could go to this wonderful place called heaven if they would only say a simple prayer, most agreed.

The prayer would essentially lead the children to say that they were sorry for the wrong things they had done. They would thank God that Jesus had died for them and their sins, and then they'd ask God to forgive them and ask Jesus to come into their hearts to help them be good boys and girls. After they said such a prayer, we all rejoiced that these little souls had become Christians and would enjoy eternity with God as their loving Father in heaven.

But what *really* came next for these children? Their family members' feelings about Christianity could be friendly, indifferent, suspicious, or even hostile. After the summer camp, they went back to their homes with their little New Testament Bibles, back to their respective cultures, and the summer program receded into memory. It's possible that such an experience could change a child's life dramatically and he or she would remain a devout Christian for life. However, it is commonly believed that only three to six percent of people who make such decisions experience permanent change. Unless something significant happened later in these children's lives, chances are that their experiences at the summer program would have little long-term impact. The invitations and prayers would soon be forgotten, provided they even understood what it had meant to invite Jesus into their hearts in the first place.

There are various theories about whether those who accept Jesus Christ this way end up in heaven or hell if nothing else happens. A prevalent theory is that God would never give up on them and that, in love, God would pursue each one for life. God would call them back into a Christian life through various circumstances such as crises, meeting roommates in college, fellow workers, or relatives who are Christians.

One way or another, God would keep calling until they return to the fold.

Indeed, this was true for a family friend. We used to babysit Jacky. She became quite close to us. When she was older, the roles reversed and she babysat our children. We sometimes took her to church. One day, when my wife, Kathy, was discussing Jesus Christ with her, she led Jacky in prayer to accept Jesus Christ as her Lord and Savior. We were all very excited. We remained friends over the years with her and her parents and even attended her wedding. However, we didn't know whether Jacky remained in her faith.

> From a human perspective, the biggest single factor in a person's eternal destiny isn't faith but heritage or the demographics of where that person lives or grows up.

Fast forward thirty years. In a recent conversation, Kathy found out that Jacky still called herself a Christian but that she had no memory of accepting Jesus Christ into her life through prayer with Kathy. As far as Jacky was concerned, she became a Christian as a result of witnessing from a university friend. We are glad and thank God for again reaching out to Jacky as an adult.

Some theories go further. Many teach that, for those who are born again, regardless of whether they exhibit visible evidence of being a Christian afterward, God welcomes these "saved" souls into His kingdom when their earthly lives are over. As long as they are sincere in inviting Jesus into their hearts, eternal life with God is assured. Dallas Willard calls this "barcode Christianity". Those who have prayed in sincerity receive a barcode for heaven. It doesn't matter what they've done before or will do after the prayer; after they die, God scans them. Those with the right barcode go to heaven and those without the barcode are tossed into hell.[5] This teaching promotes salvation through faith in Christ alone. There's a total disconnect between faith and deeds.

As I thought through these various teachings, I became confused. What if siblings of the born-again child didn't come to camp? They could lead similar or very different lives. But since they didn't have the fortunate opportunity to ask Jesus into their hearts at camp, if nothing else happened to offer them similar opportunities later in life, they would go to hell when their earthly life was over. The same logic would apply to the whole family.

When we analyze this doctrine in some detail, we're forced to come to the conclusion that what leads a soul to everlasting bliss in heaven or eternal torment in hell seems to depend more on circumstance than on anything else. For example, people who are born into cultures with no Christian influence most likely end up in hell because there are few opportunities to be born again. Those who are born into Christian families likely end up in heaven because there are generous opportunities to receive Christ.

From a human perspective, the biggest single factor in a person's eternal destiny isn't faith, but heritage or the demographics of where that person lives or grows up. It's a matter of probability. This isn't a new problem. Almost any Christian wonders sooner or later about what happens to those who live in cultures or places without a Christian presence, those who never have an opportunity to hear about Jesus Christ.

The traditional answers to such questions all point to the sovereignty of God. If I wanted to be cynical, I could say that heaven and hell are like riches and poverty. If you were born into a rich family, you'd likely stay rich. If you were born in the ghetto, you'd likely stay poor. If you were born into a Christian family, there's a high chance that your parents or someone around you would introduce you to the sinner's prayer. You then get the right barcode and go to heaven when you die. If you were born into a culture with little Christian influence or into a culture hostile to Christianity, you would likely end your earthly life with no chance of being born again.

When I questioned this logic, the typical answer was that God, in His wisdom, knew best. We were to leave things like this up to His sovereignty.

For almost a quarter of a century, I accepted this answer as legitimate, although there was a little voice in the back of my mind that wondered what God was really like. I'd learned about God's love and learned to love Him back—even if just a little. The "sovereignty of God" answer somehow seemed foreign to the God I had grown to know personally.

Every time I thought about all those people in India and the Middle East, for example, I returned to that same old question: what about those who haven't heard? Would God really condemn them to hell on account of the families they were born into or where they were raised? Unfortunately, in the narrow world I lived in, the "sovereignty of God" answer was the only way out. I learned to bury this nagging question. I kept telling myself that I just needed to trust God's unknowable wisdom.

AFRICAN KIDS

In 2001 I joined a prominent organization in which Christians from different churches and denominations worked together, including Baptists, Anglicans, Roman Catholics, Orthodox, and many other Protestant denominations. I met Chuck, a senior manager in the organization. He became a Christian as an adult, just as I had. He became a zealous evangelist after his conversion and eventually led more of his family to become Christians. After some years he started to wonder about the same questions as Scott had wondered. When he started to voice his opinions, he was met with hostility from other Christians, including his family, whom he had introduced to Christianity.

On behalf of our agency, Chuck went on a business trip to a remote part of Africa to visit a relief and development project. The people in that village were extremely poor, had little food and sustenance, and were on the verge of starvation. They deliberately slept during the day and tried to stay awake at night; it got so cold at night that if the children went to sleep, some who were weak might never wake up. The parents kept the children up all night by making them sing. When the sun came up and the temperature rose, the parents let the children sleep, hoping for a better chance that their sons and daughters would survive.

These people were so out of touch with the rest of the world, so mired in the most basic struggle for life, that the last thing on their minds was to accept Jesus Christ as Savior and Lord through a sinner's prayer. They needed food and water. They needed clothing. They needed a cup of water and a mouthful of food just to last another day.

One night, Chuck sat outside the village and told God that if he would condemn such people to hell simply for not becoming born again in this lifetime, Chuck didn't want to know Him. Through a more traumatic journey, Chuck arrived at the same question Scott asked: would God really condemn such people to hell?

Chuck told me that his family, whom he had led to the Lord when he was an evangelistic zealot, disapproved of his conclusion. In fact, he met significant opposition from his entire Christian sphere of influence. When I first joined the organization, I was warned by another senior manager that Chuck had "some weird theology."

Some Christians aren't very receptive to those who interpret the Bible differently.

THE START OF A DELIGHTFUL JOURNEY

When I discussed my question with Malcolm, a friend who had been a devout evangelical Christian longer than I, he shared that he had the same questions.

"It doesn't add up," Malcolm said to me. "The Bible says that the Lord is patient so that all can come to repentance. We also know that the vast majority of all humankind never heard about Jesus Christ. Even right now, billions of the world's people have no opportunity to pray the sinner's prayer. That means the more patient God is, the more are destined for hell. Well, this just doesn't add up!"

Scott, Chuck, and Malcolm were all godly. They loved God and people. They weren't arrogant. They were intelligent. I respected them as friends, as colleagues, and as Christians. Knowing that these God-loving, sincere, and intelligent fellow Christians were questioning what I had regarded as nonnegotiable biblical truths allowed me to ask the questions I had been afraid to ask for *decades*. Billions of people have not been born again in accordance with the sinner's prayer formula. So I ask again, what about those who haven't heard about Jesus Christ?

When I shared my questions and findings with friends, their reactions were mostly encouraging, but a few felt threatened. For example, a friend forwarded some of my questions to his seminary professor, who accused me of "watering down God's righteousness and holiness." Many held on dearly to traditional evangelical doctrines and viewed differing doctrines with suspicion, if not hostility.

One day, while reading Oswald Chambers' *My Utmost for His Highest*, I came across this entry:

> Certainty is the mark of the commonsense life—gracious uncertainty is the mark of the spiritual life. To be certain of God means that we are uncertain in all our ways.... When we become simply a promoter or a defender of a particular belief, something within us dies. That is not believing in God—it is only believing our belief about him.[6]

> *When we become simply a promoter or a defender of a particular belief, something within us dies. That is not believing in God—it is only believing our belief about him."*
> —*Oswald Chambers*

Through teachings such as these and encouragement from friends, I sought the Bible for alternatives. In addition to personal Bible studies, reading books, and having discussions with anyone who would listen to or speak with me, I enrolled and completed the core requirements of a Master of Theological Studies degree at Toronto's Tyndale University and Seminary. I was so concerned about falling into heresy that I wanted to put myself under spiritual and academic supervision.

I discovered that there had always been significant variance in biblical interpretation throughout the history of Christianity. Debates over important doctrines have raged for centuries. For example, strong opinions have been expressed for the doctrine of predestination and the opposing doctrine of free will. I found many opinions, but no consensus. Such debates are the norm rather than the exception.

My studies showed that there were biblically sound alternative answers to what I had been taught. By not insisting on a judge-first view of God, two consistent patterns emerged. One pattern led to a consistent view of God as judge; the alternative pattern led to a consistent view of God as parent.

These alternatives became forks in the road, deepening my understanding of God.

My opening question wouldn't be answered for many years, but it led me to my first discovery—the first fork in the road—right there in the first book of the Bible. The scene was Eden, where the first sin took place.

What About God's Sentence of Judgement in Genesis?

TWO

THE STORY OF THE FIRST DISOBEDIENCE IN EDEN

Let's start from the very beginning,
A very good place to start.
When you read you begin with A-B-C.
When you sing you begin with Do-Re-Me.[7]

When we discuss Christianity, we begin with Genesis, the Garden of Eden, the original sin, and its consequences. When I started to question my well-established answer to the all-important issue of the reason for the life, death, and resurrection of Jesus Christ, I decided to go back to the very beginning. I wanted to study the record of the first sin as though I were reading it for the first time, disregarding traditional interpretations as much as I could. I wanted to see what the Bible text itself says in Genesis 2–3.

Essentially, God created Adam and Eve in His own image and placed them in the Garden of Eden. It was a wonderful place where all their needs were provided for, and God related to them as their loving parent. Although God is spirit, he manifested Himself in such a way that Adam and Eve could relate to Him physically. Everything in the Garden was there for Adam and Eve to care for and enjoy, except for the fruit from the Tree of Knowledge of Good and Evil. God said, "For when you eat of it you will surely die" (Genesis 2:17).

However, the serpent tempted Eve. She took the fruit, ate it, and shared it with Adam. They then realized they were naked, and for the first time they saw the need to cover themselves at their groins, thus inventing the fashion industry. God came to visit them, but they hid. When God confronted them, Adam blamed Eve and God, and Eve blamed the serpent.

THE JUDGE-FIRST VIEW:
DID GOD ESTABLISH A DEATH SENTENCE?

Numerous Bible scholars have written about this account. Generally, they agree that God pronounced a sentence (or punishment) for eating the forbidden fruit: death. Death was the judgment God promised if Adam and Eve were to disobey Him. God established a law and the penalty for breaking it.

Most Christians agree that the Bible teaches about two kinds of death—the death of the body and the death of the spirit, or soul. Humans, starting with Adam and Eve, were created to be beings with eternal souls who related to God as their Creator and Father. In addition to physical life, a person's spirit is alive if he or she has a loving relationship with God. On the contrary, the spirit is dead if the person doesn't have a loving relationship with God or if the relationship comes to an end. Most Bible teachers and commentaries teach that when Adam and Eve disobeyed and committed the first sin, they died both physically and spiritually as a judgment from God—a "punishment of disobedience."[8] Although physical death didn't come immediately, Adam and Eve eventually died. Their spiritual death occurred immediately, however, because their loving relationship with God was broken.

Traditional teaching says that the consequence of sin, as ordained by God, was separation from Him, because a holy and righteous God couldn't accept sin and sinners in His presence. Therefore, when spiritual death occurred, Adam and Eve couldn't enjoy God's presence any longer. According to common teaching, God delivered His sentence for disobedience when he told Adam, "For in the day that you eat from it you will surely die" (Genesis 2:17, NASB).

Many teach that because God is holy and pure, He couldn't have a relationship with sinners. Therefore, God had to terminate His loving relationship with Adam and Eve. In other words, God pronounced the death sentence as a consequence. After Adam and Eve ate the forbidden fruit, God kept His promise and carried out the death sentence. In addition to keeping Adam and Eve from living forever, God also turned away from them, thereby terminating all fellowship as penalty for their disobedience. The termination of the eternal loving relationship between God and humankind is commonly known among Christians as "the second death."

But let's dig more deeply.

WHO TERMINATED THE LOVING RELATIONSHIP?

If we try to read the Genesis passage as though we're reading it for the first time, without coloring it with past interpretations, we may find it unnecessary to interpret that it was God who broke off the relationship. Let's look at the story in some detail.

Since God knows everything—an ignorant god is no God at all—he must have known that Adam and Eve had disobeyed Him. The Bible tells us that God then came into the Garden in the cool of the evening. Adam and Eve heard Him coming, became afraid, and hid from God. God asked, "Where are you?"

Who was seeking whose fellowship? Who was hiding from whom?

We can compare this to our own family experiences. In the evening, when I come home from work, I often call from the door, "Where are you?" or "Is anybody home?" I know my family is home, but I haven't seen them yet. Seeking their company and announcing my presence, I call out to them. We can see, then, that God came into the Garden and called out to Adam and Eve, seeking their fellowship.

Adam and Eve, after they ate the fruit, realized for the first time that they were naked. They decided to cover themselves. Then, in the cool of the evening, when God came looking for them, they hid.

This was a pivotal moment in the relationship between humanity and God. For the first time, Adam and Eve, the first humans, became afraid of God. The perfect loving relationship God had established between Himself and the human race came to an end. In 1 John 4:18, the Bible says, "There is no fear in love; but perfect love casts out fear, because fear involves torment. But he who fears has not been made perfect in love" (NKJV).

Adam and Eve had been living in a perfect loving relationship with God. They had no fear of Him. But when they became afraid, the loving relationship ended. Adam and Eve ended their spiritual life not so much when they disobeyed, but when they hid from God's presence. We know God didn't intend to end their fellowship because he still sought them out. Adam and Eve hid from God's desire for fellowship. They brought death to the loving relationship.

DEATH, SENTENCE, OR WARNING?

This prompts me to ask, did God really pronounce death as a punishment for disobedience? I don't think so. If I were to tell my children, "If you run across a six-lane highway during rush hour, you shall surely get run over," I wouldn't be passing a sentence on them. Neither would I be announcing a punishment for disobedience. It would be more like a prediction, a warning, or a deterrent.

God, being all wise, knew what would happen to their relationship. He knew the loving relationship between them would be broken. He knew spiritual death would surely happen. But this death wasn't the consequence of God, as judge, pronouncing a sentence for disobedience. This death was the result of one party turning away from the loving relationship. God didn't curse Adam and Eve and the human race. He had warned them what would happen if they were to disobey.

From reading the Bible, I find it difficult to accept that God imposed death of relationship between Himself and the human race. Adam and Eve were the ones who broke off the relationship. They became afraid of God. They withdrew from fellowship with God and hid. They killed their relationship with God as their loving parent. Adam and Eve didn't act in ignorance without forewarning; they were responsible for their actions.

A loving relationship requires at least two parties. If we believe Adam and Eve died spiritually when they terminated their loving relationship with God, we must remember that God initiated and shared this relationship with Adam and Eve out of love. When this relationship died, the impact extended beyond Adam and Eve. It extended to God also. If we believe Adam and Eve experienced death when this relationship ended, we need to question what God experienced as the loving parent. Is it possible for God, having been an integral part of this relationship, to have experienced death as a result of the end of His relationship with Adam and Eve?

Oswald Chambers, in *My Utmost for His Highest*, reputably the most popular Christian devotional, expresses the same concept:

> If sin rules in me, God's life in me will be killed; if God rules in me, sin in me will be killed. There is nothing more fundamental than that. The culmination of sin was the crucifixion of Jesus Christ, and what was true in the history of God on earth will also be true in your history and in mine—that is, sin will kill the life of God in us.[9]

> *"Sin will kill the life of God in us."*
> *—Oswald Chambers*

God lives in us through the Holy Spirit. Some call God's life in Christians "the indwelling of the Holy Spirit." The Holy Spirit isn't the impersonal universal Force in *Star Wars*. He's a living, feeling Person, one of the three dimensions of God expressed through the Trinity. When we sin, Chambers says that we kill the life of God in us. I agree.

God is eternal; God never dies. Therefore, it would be a stretch to say that Adam and Eve caused God's death. However, if we could turn away from our human-centric perspective and try to understand God's perspective, even if just a tiny bit, we could see that God experienced the pain of the death of this loving relationship.

We are not God. We do not love perfectly. All of us love imperfectly. No matter how much we love someone, we always withhold a little bit for self-protection. There is always some point, when we are forsaken, when we could say, "Enough is enough!" and withdraw our love. But God isn't like us. God loves perfectly and totally.

We also know that the more we love, the more we hurt when we're forsaken. That's why we all withhold a part of us when we love. The more we love, the more vulnerable we become. The more vulnerable we become, the more it hurts when our love is spurned or betrayed.

God loves without holding back. God loves with complete vulnerability. I don't think any human is capable of understanding the depth of God's pain when we spurn or betray Him. I don't think any of us could know the depth of God's pain when Adam and Eve disobeyed and turned away from Him.

God, in His wisdom, wasn't surprised by what Adam and Eve had done. He knew what would happen when Adam and Eve sinned. He announced to Adam and Eve the consequence of their sin, not as a curse but as a warning. *Knowing* is not the same as *causing*; *warning* is not the same as *sentencing*. When Adam and Eve chose to disobey, they brought about the consequences.

THE PARENT-FIRST VIEW: QUESTIONING A LIFELONG BELIEF

I was taught that death was God's punishment for Adam and Eve (and the whole human race) for the Original Sin of eating the forbidden fruit. Many books and sermons taught me about God's pronouncement of the "Adamic Curse" upon the human race. My whole understanding of the Bible and Christianity was based on God's punishment.

Unwilling to leave us in our sinful state, God put into place a plan for redemption before the creation of heaven and earth.[10] God expressed His love for us through Jesus Christ, the Lamb of God, to take our punishment.[11] His power to save us was demonstrated in the resurrection of the Son of God. This understanding depends on a very basic doctrine: God must punish sin in humans before he can have a loving relationship with them.

Or so I thought.

After studying the Genesis passage, I was startled to see that there was an alternative to understanding the account of the Original Sin and its immediate consequences. After a quarter of a century of reading the Bible almost daily, I was able to see this passage in a different light. It wasn't necessarily a story about God punishing Adam and Eve and humankind for disobedience.

I was afraid to go further.

My whole belief system as a Christian had been based on the necessity of God's punishment for sins and the belief that it had all started in Eden in Genesis 3. God had had to remove the human race from loving fellowship with Himself. God had determined the consequence of death as a result of disobedience. It broke His heart that we disobeyed, but God had to do what God had to do to uphold His holiness, justice, and righteousness.

But wait. Says who? When I put aside the *human* teaching about this Bible passage, the text spoke to me in a very different way: God hadn't initiated the death of the relationship; Adam and Eve had! If God didn't initiate it, how could I say that God was the judge who imposed death as a punishment? I couldn't find any evidence that God as judge established the death sentence for disobedience, nor could I find any evidence of God carrying out a death sentence. Quite the contrary: it was Adam and Eve who brought death to the relationship. Adam and Eve terminated life with God by spurning the loving relationship they shared with Him. In contrast to Adam and Eve's actions, God still showed up at the Garden seeking their fellowship, even after their disobedience.

I'm a father of two, a son and a daughter. I love Jason and Irene. They're both adults now and we have a good relationship. I understand how parents love their children unconditionally. Jason and Irene don't have to be perfect for me to love them and seek their fellowship. There's no question that when they disobeyed as children, my wife and I were disappointed and felt hurt. But imagine how much more deeply it would have hurt if my children had not only disobeyed, but also cut off their relationship with us. If one of our children goes for a long time without contacting us, my wife keeps reaching for the phone to call.

Loving relationship is of utmost importance between a loving parent and child. The psalmist wrote in Psalm 89:14: "Righteousness and justice are the foundation of your throne; love and faithfulness go

> *The Original Sin wasn't just the eating of fruit: it also included pride, playing the blame game, defensiveness, and rebellion.*

before you." We encounter God's love and faithfulness before we encounter His righteousness and justice. What if God's primary response to Adam and Eve wasn't to maintain His righteousness and justice but to express His love and faithfulness?

What if there was no Adamic Curse resulting in eternal punishment, but rather a Grand Plan to restore the loving relationship that Adam and Eve terminated? I wanted to discover what the Bible had to say. I started to read the rest of the Bible with the understanding that it was Adam and Eve who had brought death to the loving relationship, introducing death into the human race.

God didn't impose death as a sentence or punishment. Rather, God has been on the path of reconciliation and restoration *from the beginning*. In addition to the plan of redemption that was in place before the creation of the world, God demonstrated His reconciling love in seeking out Adam and Eve that fateful evening in the Garden, knowing they had already disobeyed Him. Furthermore, he gave them the opportunity to confess and reconcile by asking, "Who told you that you were naked? Have you eaten from the tree of which I commanded you that you should not eat?" (Genesis 3:11, NKJV)

Instead of confessing, apologizing, or seeking forgiveness and reconciliation, Adam started the first domestic quarrel in history by blaming Eve. He even accused God by blaming Him for giving him Eve. If looks could kill, I can only imagine the look Eve gave Adam when he blamed her for his own action.

The Original Sin wasn't just the eating of the fruit; it also included pride, playing the blame game, defensiveness, and rebellion. It included the first death in history, the death that the first humans *and God* had to experience: the termination of the love relationship between God and humankind.

So, what about God's sentence in Eden? *There was no sentence.* There was only a heart-wrenching warning from a loving and wise parent to His children—a warning that was ignored.

THE FORK IN THE ROAD

Finding an alternative to this common question at the very beginning of the Bible poses an interesting challenge. What would happen to the way I read the rest of the Bible?

There was a fork in the road. One choice pointed to the traditional interpretation of a judge who announced a sentence for disobedience. The other choice led to the alternative interpretation of a parent giving a warning for sin.

Would there be other forks? How many alternative answers would there be? If I were to read the rest of the Bible without the preconceived view of God as judge, what would happen to my relationship with Him?

After studying the biblical account of the Original Sin and its consequences, we're faced with a choice. I choose the path that leads to the parent. What do you choose? The path that leads to a parental God or the path that leads to a judgemental God?

As I continued my studies, I found other "What about…?" questions, each representing other forks in the road. The next such question pertains to the rest of Genesis 3, which includes more of God's response to Adam and Eve and concludes with their expulsion from the Garden of Eden.

What About the Punishments in Genesis 3?

THREE

In Genesis 2 we discovered the first fork in the road. It's biblically sound to understand God's words, "For when you eat of it you will surely die," as a warning, not a death sentence. When we choose to interpret His words as a warning, we see God as a heartbroken parent who suffers from the death of the loving relationship he shared with His beloved children, who not only disobeyed but also turned away from the relationship in fear, defensiveness, and blame.

THE JUDGE-FIRST VIEW

Genesis 3 describes a series of pronouncements from God usually interpreted as further God-ordained punishments and curses, a natural and predictable outcome of the prevalent judge-first view of God that includes two major doctrines. One is that God cannot entertain the presence of sin. Therefore, all sinners—the whole of humankind—are unacceptable in His presence unless they are made sinless. The other doctrine teaches that a just God must maintain justice by punishing all sins regardless of how trivial or terrible the acts are.

These two doctrines drove the traditional interpretation of the entire Bible for centuries. In fact, the view of a God who must punish anything and anyone for whatever displeases Him is common among most cultures and religions. When something unfortunate happens to us, our instinctive response is to wonder what we've done wrong to deserve such a fate. As a result, we often feel that God is behind what happens to us.

When unpleasant things happen, our first thought is, *Why does God let this happen to me? What have I done wrong to deserve this?* This is especially true when natural disasters such as earthquakes, hurricanes, and tsunamis hit. On March 11, 2011, a 9.0-magnitude earthquake struck Japan's east coast, triggering a massive tsunami and nuclear meltdown that resulted in widespread devastation, the loss of over twenty-eight thousand lives, and the displacement of many from their homes. The mayor of Tokyo told reporters a few days later that the tsunami was "punishment from heaven" because of the Japanese people's greed.

That pronouncement isn't unique. The same happened after the devastating tsunami that hit Indonesia and surrounding area on December 26, 2004. I've heard some Christian preachers claim that it was God's judgment against a predominantly Muslim country. These comments are ignorant and cruel. Nonetheless, they represent our tendency to attribute unpleasant events and tragedies to God. By doing this we imply that God allows certain unpleasant things to happen—or even instigates them—to punish us for our sins.

Most Bible students interpret the consequences in Genesis 3 along a similar vein. Adam and Eve disobeyed. God was displeased. As a result, he excluded them from His presence by chasing them out of Eden, making life a whole lot harder through various punishments.

LET'S DIG MORE DEEPLY

If we agree based on the first fork in the road that there's a legitimate and biblical basis for a parent-first view of God, we may discover another fork in the immediate aftermath of the Original Sin. At this fork, we can again choose between viewing God as the judge or as the parent.

Read Genesis 3:14–24 as though you're reading it for the first time with what we've learned so far as a context. Think of a heartbroken parent setting up a plan of redemption to limit the impact of sin and restore loving relationships without turning His children into mindless robots or slaves, but rather willing participants.

THE WHOLE CREATION HAS CHANGED

Life on earth took a drastic change when Adam and Eve ate the fruit from the Tree of the Knowledge of Good and Evil. I don't think anyone is capable of understanding the full impact or meaning of this change. For example, why was nakedness okay before they ate and not okay immediately after? Was it because they threw off the covering of God's love and felt vulnerable? Further, why did Adam and Eve cover their groins, the location of the sexual organs, of all places? There has been much speculation about this, but the Bible doesn't really explain. Sigmund Freud, founder of psychoanalysis and famous for his research into human sex drives, could have had a field day.

> *After the Garden humans loved themselves more than they loved anything or anyone else. Life was no longer as God had planned.*

One thing I do understand, however, is the death of the loving relationship Adam and Eve brought between humankind and God—and between themselves. Adam blamed Eve for giving him the fruit, then blamed God for giving him Eve. Eve blamed the serpent for tempting her. No one accepted responsibility for disobedience. I see no apologies or repentance. Consequently, through the brokenness of relationships, death reigned.

From this point onward, without restoration, physical life continued without the more important spiritual life. Just like a physically dead person cannot give birth, Adam and Eve couldn't pass on to their offspring what they had discarded: a loving spiritual relationship with God.

The result is that humans no longer love selflessly, as God intended. After the Garden, humans loved themselves more than they loved anything or anyone else. Life was no longer as God had planned.[12]

Self-gratification caused Adam and Eve to eat the fruit from the Tree of the Knowledge of Good and Evil. We read in Genesis 3:6:

When the woman saw that the fruit of the tree was good for food and pleasing to the eye, and also desirable for gaining wisdom, she took some and ate it. She also gave some to her husband, who was with her, and he ate it. (TNIV)

The act was motivated by gratifying the self. Its appearance was appealing and one would gain wisdom for the mind, fulfilling the desire to be like God (Genesis 3:5).

We also learned that Adam and Eve responded to the situation with fear, defensiveness, and blame, not repentance, vulnerability, or accountability. Selfish motivations were the rule for interactions with God and between Adam and Eve. This propensity was passed on to the rest of the human race. The primary motive for every human descendant was not selfless love, but self-love. The impact of this self-driven physical life was felt soon thereafter with the murder of Abel by Cain (Genesis 4:1–9). Strife and enmity continue to poison relationships among humans, families, tribes, cultures, and nations to this day.

Since God created humans in His image, we're still capable of loving, but this love has been fatally poisoned by self-love. Although we're called to love one another—and we *are* capable of loving to some extent—very few of us can claim to have loved to the fullest. The world God created still exists, but it has changed for the worse. It's been infected by an illness called sin—our willful desire to love ourselves more than others.

God intended for us to live a life of mutual love in which we do what's best for one another, with God as our loving parent. We became incapable of practicing mutual love as our basic motivation. Now, we have to overcome self-love before we can love others. History shows that most of us haven't been able to consistently overcome self-love. Instead, most of us wouldn't hesitate to gratify ourselves at a cost to others. Some carry this out to murderous degrees. The world is far from God's intended love-filled creation. It's been badly damaged by sin.

Adolf Hitler was one of the cruelest dictators in recent centuries. Millions perished in anguish, in horrible violence during World War II. It's unimaginable that someone like him could have the potential to live forever. The same goes for others, both living and dead. They cause untold misery through greed, hunger for power, pride, bigotry, and racism.

If we're honest with ourselves and examine our feelings and motives before God, we have to admit that we are filled with our own ugly intentions. We may never have the opportunity to inflict harm as severely as the Hitlers of the world, but those who are introspective will admit that we have caused our own share of misery and hurt on others. If we had eternal physical life in our current state, life on earth for most of us would become a never-ending nightmare. Some would call it hell.

God, true to His love as our parent, would do anything to rescue us from this hell. And God does.

THE PARENT-FIRST VIEW:
GOD'S LIMITATION OF ETERNAL EVIL

In Genesis 3:14–19, God pronounces a series of predictions. Most interpret these as curses, as punishments put in place by God. However, I want to point out two things. First, there's no mention of eternity. No matter how one interprets this passage, it's unnecessary to extend the pronouncements to eternity. Life on earth has inherited the legacy of sin and resultant harm and suffering. Whether this extends to eternity is uncertain. Second, this series of pronouncements is discipline from a loving parent intent on training his children, not penalties that a judge would impose in retribution.

God knew that life on earth wasn't going to be as he had intended, but he had a plan to reconcile this mess back to a love-based creation. Philip Yancey wrote an amazingly succinct "plot" for the Bible:

A single family of nomads migrates into Egypt, becomes a large tribe, escapes from slavery, then travels to their original homeland, which they must retake by force. They form a nation, which flourishes for a brief time and then divides in two and succumbs to attacks by its larger neighbors. After several centuries pass, the emerging empires of Greece and then Rome conquer the territory, and in that puppet state a new prophet arises, Jesus by name, whom some see as the promised Messiah. He is executed, and a new religion forms around him, which opens up the Jewish heritage to all other races....Jesus dies and is resurrected, and as a result something permanently alters in the universe. For the first time, all people have the opportunity for peace with God. Moreover, all of human history points toward a culmination in which the Messiah will return and restore the earth to its original design.[13]

Until the restoration takes place, God in His mercy wants to limit the harm we inflict on ourselves, others, and creation. Therefore, he prevented Adam and Eve from eating the fruit from the tree of life. We read in Genesis 3:22–23:

> *And the Lord God said, "The man has now become like one of us, knowing good and evil. He must not be allowed to reach out his hand and take also from the tree of life and eat, and live forever." So the Lord God banished him from the Garden of Eden.* (TNIV)

Note that the reason for the expulsion wasn't to prevent Adam and Eve from enjoying life in Eden, but to prevent access to the tree of life, which would have enabled eternal physical life. Because of this, every human's physical existence has a time limit. I'm unsure about the reason for the gradual reduction of longevity throughout the generations, but there is nonetheless an absolute end to each human's earthly life. Those who read Revelation, the last book of the Bible, will see that the tree of life will be back in the New Jerusalem, where we'll live in perfect harmony as God intended all along. This time we'll enjoy its fruit and live forever (see Revelation 22:1-3). Until then, God limits our suffering by limiting our physical lives.

In this passage are three pronouncements from God. The first (Genesis 3:14–15) was directed toward the serpent: The serpent will crawl and eat dust, and there will be enmity between the serpent's and the woman's offspring; hers will crush the serpent's head and the serpent

The tree of life will be back in the New Jerusalem, where we'll live in perfect harmony as God intended all along.

will strike the offspring's heel. Most Christians understand this as the first mention of God's plan of redemption for fallen humanity through the defeat of evil by the offspring of Eve.

The second passage (Genesis 3:16) was directed toward Eve: The woman will experience pain in childbearing and birth. She will desire the husband, and the husband will rule over her.

The third pronouncement (Genesis 3:17–19) was directed toward Adam: Raising food from the ground will be a struggle, and Adam (and his offspring, I assume) will have a tough time making a living until we all return to dust. In general, earthly life will be tough for humankind.

I don't know whether these curses were something God deliberately and actively set in place or whether they were simply the natural consequences of disobedience. By letting us experience the hardships of a world poisoned by sin, God helps us see the futility of earthly life without perfect love and peace with Him, among ourselves, and with creation. These curses are God's way of helping us long for a better life. But there is an end to these curses.

God helps us long for the new creation he prepares for us. It doesn't mean this life isn't worth living, but we have a much better life waiting for us afterward. Paul the Apostle expresses this very well in Philippians 1:21–24:

For to me, to live is Christ and to die is gain. If I am to go on living in the body, this will mean fruitful labor for me. Yet what shall I choose? I do not know! I am torn between the two: I desire to depart and be with Christ, which is better by far; but it is more necessary for you that I remain in the body. (NIV)

Paul lived on earth for the good of others, and he also longed for a better life after his earthly life was over.

"Life is hard, and then you die." Or at least so goes a common saying. Except for a very privileged few, this is true for all humankind, and I doubt anyone, including the privileged few, would say his or her life is always perfect. We all experience hardship, some more than others, and no one can claim a perfect life. However, God does have a perfect life for us, a life we will experience when he brings total reconciliation and restoration. Until then he limits our suffering by limiting the length of our earthly lives. He lets us face the consequences of our sins so we can look forward to the better life he has in store for us.

THE FORK IN THE ROAD

In trying to understand the curses in Genesis 3 and the expulsion of Adam and Eve from Eden, we face another fork in the road of knowing God. We can see God as a judge, punishing us and keeping us from good things such as the tree of life and a life of ease *because of* our disobedience. Alternatively, we can see God as a parent limiting our suffering, which stems from our sins, and helping us hope for a better life when he fully carries out His plan of redemption *despite* our disobedience.

I choose to believe that the consequences pronounced in Genesis 3 express God's intention and plan to limit sin and its consequences. Further, God wants to help us see the temporal nature of this life so that we can set our hearts on eternity with God, when he restores all creation through the Messiah.

What's your choice?

What About the Laws in the Old Testament?

FOUR

SPEEDING TICKETS AND COMMANDS IN THE BIBLE

When my family was young, my wife and I took Jason and Irene on road trips. One evening, at the end of one of these trips, on the expressway near home, Jason asked from the backseat, "Dad, why are other drivers so slow?"

My nickname is Fast Eddie, thanks to Paul Newman in *The Color of Money*. I deserve it. One time, while driving back to Toronto after vacationing south of the border, I got two speeding tickets in one day. My wife still gasps and closes her eyes when I drive, and that's an improvement over white knuckles. In my younger days, speeding tickets were my regular punishment for impatient and aggressive driving.

Many traffic experts, however, agree that Canada's expressway speed limits are unrealistically low. Studies have shown that eighty to eighty-five percent of drivers on expressways exceed the speed limit by more than ten percent. On Highway 401, which runs through Toronto, the speed limit is one hundred kilometers (sixty-two miles) per hour. During off-peak hours, when traffic flows freely, it's difficult to drive in the passing lanes under 120 kph (75 mph) without resulting in a string of cars backed up behind you, tailgating, flashing their high beams, passing on the right, and giving you one-finger salutes.

THE JUDGE-FIRST VIEW

To a certain extent, that was the way I used to look at the Bible's numerous commands, especially those in Old Testament books like Exodus, Leviticus, and Deuteronomy. In the New Testament, Jesus' famous Sermon on the Mount also contains strict teachings, such as gouging out your eyes or cutting off your limbs if they cause you to sin.[14] It's impossible for anyone to claim that he or she has followed every command in the Bible.

The Bible contains teachings that seem to make it difficult to excuse transgressions. For example, many Christians frequently quote verses such as "All have sinned and fall short of the glory of God" (Romans 3:23), "For the wages of sin is death" (Romans 6:23), and "Whoever keeps the whole law and yet stumbles at just one point is guilty of breaking all of it" (James 2:10). These are meant to demonstrate that we all violate laws in the Bible.

According to this teaching, God's requirements for righteousness and purity are so absolute and numerous that it would be impossible for anyone to meet His standard: perfect sinlessness. I doubt any driver can claim to have *never* exceeded the speed limit. The same is true with God's laws. No one can claim to have obeyed them all. Although we can exceed speed limits with impunity most of the time, God is omniscient and knows our every act. Therefore, at the end of the day, every human is without excuse. No one can claim to be sinless before God. And since God demands one hundred percent purity before allowing us into His presence, something must be done to remove our sin before we can enjoy His presence in eternity. This teaching is especially popular among evangelical Christians.

There is a common explanation in the Bible for all these commands and it goes something like this: God is holy, righteous, and just. We are sinful and hopelessly lost. We are prideful and refuse to admit our sinfulness and need for God's forgiveness and acceptance. Through His laws God wants to prove our inability to obey Him. God never expects us frail and sinful human beings to keep up with His standard. The laws are proof that we'll always fall short of God's holiness, righteousness, and justice. They show that we're incapable of loving God and others as God calls us to without His enablement and strength. God wants to create in us a sense of desperate and humble dependency on Him. Through these laws God wants to drive us to the realization that we're hopelessly lost without His rescue. In other words, a major reason for God's commands is to prove that we can't keep them.[15]

This teaching shows that keeping the laws of God is a hopeless endeavor without God's grace. We desperately need God to forgive us of our transgressions, and we must depend on God to give us strength to live even a semblance of a godly life.

LET'S DIG MORE DEEPLY

If I were to take a somewhat cynical point of view, it would seem to me that God needs to prove we're failures without Him. Since there's no chance in a million years that any of us could live up to His standards of holiness, righteousness, and justice, it would seem he sets us up for failure by giving us rules and regulations with the full knowledge that we can never keep up. I know this seems harsh, but this is the implication of accepting that God commands us to follow all these rules and regulations with the knowledge that we could never live up to them. We are deserving of His punishment.

GOD'S LAW: PENALTY OR OFFERING?

Someone once asked me, "What about all the punishments from God in the Bible?" I tried to find evidence in the Bible to validate the concept that God *must* punish sins. Using a computerized concordance, I searched for *p* words such as *punish, punishment, penalty,* and *penalize.* I started with the New International Version. The first two occurrences of a *p* word—*penalty*—turned up in Leviticus 5 and 6.

> *If a person sins because he does not speak up when he hears a public charge to testify regarding something he has seen or learned about, he will be held responsible...When anyone is guilty in any of these*

ways, he must confess in what way he has sinned and, as a penalty
*for the sin he has committed, he must bring to the Lord a female
lamb or goat from the flock as a sin offering.... If he cannot afford
a lamb, he is to bring two doves or two young pigeons to the Lord
as a penalty for his sin
...If, however, he cannot afford two doves or two young pigeons, he
is to bring as an offering for his sin a tenth of an ephah [about two
quarts or two liters] of fine flour for a sin offering.*
(Leviticus 5:1–11, emphasis added)

*The Lord said to Moses: "If anyone sins and is unfaithful to the
Lord by deceiving his neighbor about something entrusted to him
or left in his care or stolen...he must return what he has stolen or
taken by extortion...or whatever it was he swore falsely about. He
must make restitution in full, add a fifth of the value to it and give
it all to the owner on the day he presents his guilt offering. And as
a* penalty *he must bring to the priest, that is, to the Lord, his guilt
offering.... In this way the priest will make atonement for him
before the Lord, and he will be forgiven for any of these things he
did that made him guilty."*
(Leviticus 6:1–7, emphasis added)

> *To my surprise, I
> couldn't find the word*
> penalty *in
> the same passages in these
> versions. Instead, I found
> the terms,* guilt offering
> *and* sin offering.

When I found these passages in the
NIV Bible, I thought my search was
over. These passages clearly describe
the consequences of the transgressions
God ordains as *penalties* that must be
presented to Him through the sacrificial
system, just like paying speeding
tickets through the court system. If the
Israelites broke any laws, they had to
pay a *penalty* to God.

To be thorough, I did a similar search using other translations: the
New American Standard Bible (NASB), the New King James Version
(NKJV), and the Amplified Bible (AMP). To my surprise I couldn't

find the word *penalty* in the same passages in these versions. Instead, I found the terms *guilt offering* and *sin offering*.

Further, in searching the whole Bible for the *p* words, I turned out more surprises. The NIV uses English words based on *punish* and *penalty* thirty-one percent more often than the NASB and fifty-three percent more frequently than the NKJV. This told me that some words in Hebrew and Greek may or may not mean exactly *punishment* or *penalty*. The choice of the *p* words depends on the translators' interpretation of not only the word itself but also their personal or collective bias and understanding of the context.

This finding may not surprise a serious Bible student, but this was early on in my journey. At that time I thought there was relative uniformity among Bible translators. I thought the different translations presented the same meanings and differed only in grammar and style of presentation. But it seemed to me that *penalty* and *offering* had vastly different meanings.

I decided to dig more deeply. I referred to Bible dictionaries, seeking the meaning of the original Hebrew words. I found that *punishment* or *penalty* represented only one of the possible meanings. In fact, the word was translated as other meanings *more often*. In these two passages in Leviticus, the NASB, AMP, and NKJV translators used the terms *guilt offering* or *sin offering* instead of *penalty*.[16]

So, how does one decide which is the most appropriate interpretation? In thinking about it, the comparison between a bouquet of flowers and a speeding ticket comes to mind.

SAY IT WITH FLOWERS

One afternoon I took the commuter train home holding a bouquet of fresh flowers. The conductor teased me, "Looks like you're either in trouble or getting into trouble!" You see, my wife, Kathy, loves flowers. Fresh flowers always please her. When something happens that saddens her, whether it's my fault or not, I get her flowers or a flowering plant. It never fails to please her. Sometimes I do it without having to wait for a reason or an occasion.

It's especially true when I've blown it and need her forgiveness. I say it with flowers. Although she never asks for it, I know her well enough to know what pleases her. The flowers are my guilt offering. They're a sincere expression of my sorrow and intention not to repeat the offense. In other words, they show my repentance. It pleases her that I do something special, offering her something I know she likes, to express my desire to reconcile with her. But I wonder how she'd feel if I were to think of the flowers as a penalty, the same as I would think of paying a speeding ticket.

> *An offering is something I want to do in love to express my sorrow and desire to reconcile. A penalty, on the other hand, is something I have to do to stay out of trouble or avoid a consequence that's worse than the penalty.*

There's a difference between an offering and a penalty. The action may be the same in that I do something in response to an offense I've committed. But the motivations are worlds apart. In fact, I think Kathy would be heartbroken if I were to regard the flowers as a speeding ticket fine, a penalty I pay with reluctance and obligation.

I used to get together with a bunch of guys every Saturday morning for breakfast. I shared this viewpoint one morning and one of them, David, decided to give it a try. At a later Saturday breakfast, David told us that it hadn't worked for him. He'd had a disagreement with his wife and it got pretty hot. So he bought some flowers, went to her in the kitchen, threw them on the table, and said, "Here."

He was surprised it didn't work. We all had a good laugh, but it served to illustrate that even flowers don't work when they're presented as an obligation.

An offering is something I want to do in love to express my sorrow and desire to reconcile. A penalty, on the other hand, is something I have to do to stay out of trouble or avoid a consequence that's worse than the penalty.

RECONCILIATION OR PUNISHMENT?

My investigation into this translation issue caused me to look at all the rules, regulations, and commands in the Bible from a fresh perspective. What if I were to look at them from the perspective that they aren't penalties but are ways God prescribes to reconcile with Him and with the people in my life I've offended or hurt?

This idea helped me to see scripture in a fresh light. For example, Exodus 21:33–36 presents an example of how one can compensate for mistakes that have caused damage to others:

> *If a man opens a pit, or digs a pit and does not cover it over, and an ox or a donkey falls into it, the owner of the pit shall make restitution; he shall give money to its owner, and the dead animal shall become his.*
>
> *If one man's ox hurts another's so that it dies, then they shall sell the live ox and divide its price equally; and also they shall divide the dead ox. Or if it is known that the ox was previously in the habit of goring, yet its owner has not confined it, he shall surely pay ox for ox, and the dead animal shall become his.* (NASB)

When someone causes property damage, he has to repay it fairly. However, after paying, he retains the dead animal. When one ox kills another the treatment is different, depending on whether or not the owner of the offending ox has been careless. This demonstrates how, by following God's commands, the Hebrews could bring restoration through fair reconciliation. It certainly isn't punishment as such.

This is consistent with our discoveries in trying to understand God's response to sin. In chapter 2 we discovered an alternative understanding of God's fateful words in Genesis 2:16—"You shall surely die." They were meant as a warning from a loving parent rather than a sentence from an immovable judge. In chapter 3 we discovered that the other seemingly harsh responses from God in Genesis 3 were actually acts of kindness to limit our suffering and begin the plan for reconciliation. In this chapter we seek to learn from the laws and commands in Exodus, Deuteronomy, and Leviticus, all the while considering the following question: what if these laws and commandments are consistent with our discoveries so far, that they are not penalties from a judge but a continuation of God's plan of reconciliation, a plan God put into action when he walked into the Garden of Eden seeking fellowship with the guilt-ridden Adam and Eve?

When I do something wrong, when I sin, harm results. I hurt others, God, and myself. This is consistent with what happened in the Garden of Eden. When Adam blamed both Eve and God for His offense, he hurt them. God's response was to immediately lay out a plan of restoration, and the rest of the Bible further unfolds that plan. The Bible is full of teachings we can follow to restore our broken relationships through acts of repentance and reconciliation. We can look at these as penalties, or we can look at them as sincere and loving expressions of sorrow and repentance.

THE PARENT-FIRST VIEW: CHOOSING A MINDSET

If we get ourselves out of the mindset that God wants to *punish* us for the sake of His holiness, justice, and dignity, and get into the mindset that God wants to show us ways to *restore* our loving relationships with Him and with people, we might view the many laws and commandments in the Bible differently. They aren't impossible demands to show us our inability to attain God's standards in our own strength, so that we feel like failures and become desperate for His grace and power through Christ to save us from our penalty. Instead, they provide appropriate and specific means for us to show our sorrow and demonstrate repentance, so that we can reconcile with God and our neighbors, bringing us back to a loving relationship—*shalom*[17]—after we've offended them through our sins.

> *God's laws are paths to restoration from a loving parent, not demands for perfection from a stern judge.*

We desperately need God, but the reason for our desperation is not God's impossibly stringent demands or standards. Think of the Ten Commandments. There are only ten of them, but none of us can claim to have obeyed all of them at all times. On the other hand, which one of us would marry someone, hire an employee, or form a partnership with someone who claims the Ten Commandments are no good and has no intention of following any of them? Although we agree they're good, we still cannot obey even ten commands. How, then, can anyone hope to follow the hundreds that are listed in the first five books of the Bible? When we admit our inability to live in full accordance with the law, we realize our desperate need for God's sustaining power and love. Although we can come to this realization, *it's not God's intention to use these laws to prove we are failures.*

The reason for our desperation is our refusal to follow (or negligence in following) God's ways of reconciliation. Even when we admit they are appropriate—and even when it's in our power to do it—we still refuse to reconcile.[18] Many of us can recall occasions when we could have restored a relationship regardless of whose fault it was or who caused the brokenness, if only we could overcome our pride. We are, indeed, as Romans 7:13 concludes, utterly sinful. We desperately need God to rescue us from our sins because of our consistently willful refusal and careless neglect to love God and people, even when God shows us ways to reconcile with one another and with God.

This may seem like splitting hairs. However, it's important to understand the difference. This is an important fork in the road. God's commands aren't there to prove we are failures who deserve punishment, which further drives us into the mercy and grace of the Savior. Instead, God's commands represent the means by which we can avoid sinning. By following these instructions, we can reconcile with other people and God after we sin. They represent *choices*. There are many choices because we are capable of many sins. God's laws are paths to restoration from a loving parent, not demands for perfection from a stern judge.

We need to take the mindset that God desires to be on our side as a loving parent, helping us first to avoid sinning and then to reconcile with Him and others when we inevitably blow it. We need to get away from the mindset that God is high on the bench, administering inflexible justice as an immovable judge. Knowing that God helps to restore loving relationships with Him and people, we have the assurance that when we follow these God-ordained laws in faith, we can count on reconciliation.

When the laws and commandments specify how we should compensate others for our offenses, we can also be sure that the compensations are objective, sufficient, and fair—at least in the context of the culture when the laws and commandments were given. Further, since these laws were administered by priests, people could depend on a qualified and impartial third party to administer justice and reconciliation.

It's important to understand the difference between viewing God's requirements as *penalties* and viewing them as *offerings*. Although it's true that we all desperately need God, our ways of arriving at our need for God can be different. The way of penalties causes us to approach the law with an attitude of *compliance* and *grudge*. They are punishments we *have* to comply with. If we could avoid it, we would. The way of offerings, however, causes us to approach the law with an attitude of *relief* and *gratitude*. If we truly care for the people we've offended, we would bring our offerings with joy in our heart, knowing we bring something that can restore *shalom* and reconcile our loving relationships.

If I knew God would be pleased when I brought my offerings, I would look forward to presenting them. Even the act of preparing an offering would be pleasurable. I would grudgingly send a check to pay for a speeding ticket at the last possible moment to avoid facing the judge in court, but I remember having a smile on my face when presenting a bouquet I knew would please my wife.

We can also note the aspect of *affordability* of the required offerings. By following the requirements in the Leviticus 5 passage, we can see that the offering started with a female lamb or goat. For many that would have been a small fortune. If the offender couldn't afford that, two doves or young pigeons would have been sufficient. Although more affordable, the doves and pigeons could still be difficult for the poor. Ultimately, all the offender needed to bring was an offering of the equivalence of about two quarts (about two liters) of flour.[19] God ensured the offerings were affordable for the offender.

Therefore, it's unnecessary to view the laws and commandments as penalties for wrongdoings. We can choose to view them as specific ways to reconcile us back into loving relationships after we've offended God and people. We have come to understand life as the existence of loving relationships and death as the absence or end of loving relationships. The laws and commandments, therefore, are ways to lead us out of death into life. They show us the way out of broken relationships into the restoration of loving relationships.

God is on our side, and he spares no effort in showing us numerous ways to cross over from death to life, from estrangement to love. God gives us many ways to reconcile with Him and other people—ways that are specific and appropriate to the offenses committed and that will repair our broken relationships.

THE FORK IN THE ROAD

When I relate to God as Father, I don't view the laws as penalties I need to pay to appease the judge and keep myself out of trouble. I view them as specific routes on a roadmap back to the heart of the Father. We should be grateful for the many ways God has made available for us to reconcile with Him and people, instead of blaming God for giving us so many laws and commandments that are impossible to obey. God doesn't prescribe laws and commandments as penalties to prove we are failures. Instead, God shows us many ways to speak the language of love and reconciliation.

This is another fork in the road. It can lead us to the view of a loving Father who provides the roadmap, longing for the joyous return of His wayward children. He eagerly welcomes each of us with a a big grin and warm embrace. God has given His children instructions throughout the ages, and especially through the Bible, to show us how to get back to loving relationships with God and with people.

God does stipulate the consequences for breaking the law. Some have chosen to view them as penalties, as is emphasized in the NIV and NLT translations of the Bible; others have chosen to view them as offerings, as in the NASB, NKJV, and AMP translations. Your choice has a profound impact on how you relate to God. Choosing to view these consequences as penalties will take you down the road to relate to God as a judge who forces us to reach out to Him. Choosing to view them as offerings will take you down the road to relate to God as a parent who is committed to restoring loving relationships. Which do you choose?

I prefer the offering view. This doesn't mean God ignores justice. God is intensely interested in justice. But do we really understand what justice means, according to the Bible?

What About Justice
in the Bible?

FIVE

THE TRADITIONAL JUDGE-FIRST VIEW

Our church in Toronto usually had a shortage of Sunday school teachers during the summer, when many people flocked to their cottages for the weekends. My wife and I never had a cottage, and we attended church most Sundays throughout the year. I sometimes helped out in children's church during the cottage season.

One Sunday while assisting with the children's church, I heard the teacher telling the children, a couple of whom were hers, that God couldn't accept their presence because they were sinners. They had to be punished. Unless they accepted Jesus' death as payment for their sins, God wouldn't allow them into His presence.

This teaching disturbed me deeply. I was speechless. Most evangelical churches teach the same to children and adults alike. Although this sets up a simple reason for people to accept Jesus Christ, what does it communicate about God as Father? What sick parent would find it necessary to punish his or her children for every infraction? Not only that, but such a parent would also have to shut out the children forever and ever, regardless of the severity of the infraction!

I knew the teacher and her spouse well, and this wasn't the way they treated their children. In the children's subconscious minds, they must have felt that either their parents weren't good representations of God, or God the Father was a totally different kind of parent in heaven! But that's the way most evangelicals teach about God's justice.

LET'S DIG MORE DEEPLY

Biblical justice is complex. It's also one of the most important topics in the Bible. The Holman Bible Dictionary defines justice as:

> The order God seeks to reestablish in His creation where all people receive the benefits of life with Him. As love is for the New Testament, so justice is the central ethical idea of the Old Testament[20]

Christopher Marshall, an internationally recognized advocate and author on the integration of theology and criminal justice, notes:

> There are hundreds of texts in the Old and New Testament which speak explicitly about justice, and hundreds more which refer to it implicitly. Justice is in fact one of the most frequently recurring topics in the Bible....For example, the main vocabulary items for sexual sin appear about 90 times in the Bible, while the major Hebrew and Greek words for justice...occur over 1,000 times.[21]

The Bible has a lot to say about justice.

Traditionally, Western cultures have been heavily influenced by the Greeks and Romans. Similarly, our sense of justice is mainly based on Greco-Roman traditions. However, the Hebrew Bible was very *un*-Greco-Roman. Influenced by the Hebrew scriptures, the Jewish culture was very different from Greek and Roman cultures as well as from surrounding Middle Eastern and Asian cultures. In the first century, this cultural difference extended to how Jews understood justice.

Most of the first-generation Christians were Jews. Starting from the latter part of the first century, however, Gentile (non-Jewish) converts became the main thrust behind the explosive growth of Christianity around the Mediterranean. Virtually all second-generation and later Christian leaders were Gentiles from Greek, Roman, and Egyptian cultures. This dominant Gentile influence resulted in a significant impact on the development of Christian theology, including the interpretation of biblical justice.

Let's look at some well-publicized events to help us understand the complexity of justice.

A judge denied bail Wednesday for a Georgia man who was sentenced to 10 years in jail for having consensual oral sex at 17 with a 15-year-old girl—even though another judge tossed out the sentence a week earlier.

Douglas County Superior Court Judge David Emerson ruled that Genarlow Wilson—who is now 21 and has been behind bars for 27 months—will have to stay in jail at least until October.

The former honours student was convicted in 2005 of aggravated child molestation, after receiving oral sex at a New Year's Eve party in 2003. In Georgia, the age of consent is 16 and under state law at the time, a minimum 10-year sentence was mandatory for the crime.

Wilson's original sentence was widely criticized on the grounds it was grossly disproportionate to the crime. State legislators later changed the law to make the crime a misdemeanor punishable by up to a year in jail.[22]

Wilson received his freedom October 26, 2007, after the Georgia Supreme Court ruled that "his punishment was cruel, unusual, and grossly improportionate (*sic.*)."[23] He was in jail for over thirty months.

A beaming Paris Hilton strolled out of jail Tuesday after a stay of more than three weeks for violating probation on driving offences in a bizarre legal melodrama that saw the billionaire heiress set free, then returned behind bars in a stream of tears and screams.

Hilton will complete her probation in March 2009 as long as she keeps her driver's license current and doesn't break any laws.

She can reduce that time by 12 months if she does community service that could include a public-service announcement, the city attorney's office has said.

Hilton began a reduced, 23-day sentence on June 3 for violating her probation in an alcohol-related reckless driving case.

Hilton's path to jail began Sept. 7, when she failed a sobriety test after police saw her weaving down a street in her Mercedes-Benz on what she said was a late-night run to a hamburger stand.

She pleaded no contest to reckless driving and was sentenced to 36 months probation, alcohol education, and $1,500 in fines.

In the months that followed, she was stopped twice by officers who discovered her driving with a suspended license. The second stop landed her in Sauer's courtroom, where he sentenced her to jail.[24]

Judging from these contrasting news stories, it's obvious that justice is not simple. What is justice? Who decides what is just? Who decides that a teenager having consensual oral sex with a younger teenager in violation of an obsolete law deserves *forty times* more jail time than an adult repeatedly endangering herself and others by driving under the influence of drugs with a suspended license? Does having money to buy the best lawyers have anything to do with justice? Does being rich and famous contribute to special favors from our justice system? Is the color of skin or gender an issue? These aren't easy questions to answer.

Understanding biblical justice is no easier. What does justice mean to the Jews, who hold sacred the Hebrew scriptures (the Old Testament)? Does the same meaning of justice apply to Christians, who regard both the Hebrew scriptures and Greek scriptures (the New Testament) as God's word? Who interprets biblical justice for us? Does biblical justice apply to our society today or does it apply only to the Jews and the Christians?

A proper discussion of biblical justice would require more space than one chapter provides. Therefore, we'll briefly study two definitions of justice for the purpose of helping us understand how we can relate to God. One way of understanding justice will lead us to relate to God as a judge, and the other will lead us to relate to God as a parent.

TWO DEFINITIONS OF JUSTICE

Christopher Marshall, a prominent proponent of biblical justice, is the author of *Beyond Retribution*, a definitive book about New Testament justice. The book has offered me a deeper and clearer understanding of what the Bible teaches about justice.

In particular, Marshall describes two major types of justice: *retributive* justice and *restorative* justice. Retributive justice focuses on the assignment of blame and the punishment of the guilty. In other words, who started the fight? Who stole from whom? In this tradition "the question of guilt is paramount, together with the infliction of punishment upon [the guilty]."[25] On the other hand, restorative justice focuses on creating and restoring "*shalom*, a state of soundness or 'all-rightness' within the community."[26] It is "comprehensively relational."[27]

Greek and Roman cultures dominated the Mediterranean during the birth of Christianity and continue to dominate Western cultures to this day. The Greco-Roman tradition of justice was mostly retributive. Punishment was the key deterrent to breaking any law. Most leaders in the first few centuries of Christianity were scholars, nobility, and lawyers from the Greco-Roman tradition. This cultural bias caused them to interpret justice in the Hebrew Bible and teachings of Jesus Christ through the lens of retributive justice.

Under retributive justice, when someone breaks the law, justice is served if the offender is made to experience equivalent or greater harm than the offender has caused. If I made someone miserable, retributive justice is achieved when I am made equally or more miserable. From an objective viewpoint, this is odd. How are justice and fairness served when the total amount of misery is increased, when more misery is added to the offender without lessening or compensating for the misery of the victim?

> *How is justice served when more misery is added to the offender without compensating for the misery of the victim?*

Nonetheless, a fixation on retributive justice has caused most Christians since the dawn of Christianity to theorize that God's primary response to sins is punishment. To this day and especially in the Western world, many, if not most, Christians think that God must punish sinners so as to uphold justice. According to this common teaching, if God doesn't punish the guilty, God would be unjust, and God simply cannot be unjust! This teaching remains dominant in the twenty-first century, especially among American evangelicals.

Jerry Bridges is a typical evangelical proponent of retributive justice. In *The Gospel for Real Life*, Bridges writes:

> God's justice is…inflexible [and] certain….Justice may be defined as rendering to everyone according to one's due. Justice means we get exactly what we deserve—nothing more, nothing less…. God does not exalt His mercy at the expense of His justice. And in order to maintain His justice, *all sin without exception must be punished*. Contrary to popular opinion, with God there is no such thing as mere forgiveness. There is only justice.[28]

Not only is this view counterintuitive in terms of our daily experience, it's *extremely limited* in the context of true biblical justice. When we're exposed to this kind of teaching, we can be made to feel that unless we believe in a God who insists on punishing all sinners for every sin they've committed, we don't believe God is just or we claim that God doesn't uphold justice.

God *is* just. God *does* uphold justice. But biblical justice isn't just about retributive justice. One of the most distinctive purposes of the Hebrew scriptures is to differentiate between Jewish culture and the surrounding cultures. Marshall notes that, as opposed to retributive justice, the Hebrew Bible teaches *restorative* justice. Jesus taught restorative justice. Paul, a Jewish scholar and rabbi, also taught restorative justice. Under this teaching, God is committed to creating and restoring *shalom*, which means relational peace among the people and with Him. *Shalom* refers to a state of soundness or "all-rightness" within the community. *Shalom* exists when people relate to one another and with God in harmony and peace, in accordance with God's character as expressed in the Bible. Restorative justice is the purpose of God's laws.

When we read through the laws and commands in the Bible, we find that, with the exception of the Old Testament offenses that result in death (which will be addressed in a later chapter), the laws are restorative in nature. Offenders of the laws are required through compensations to restore the losses they have caused their victims. They are also required through offerings to restore their relationships with God.

As we learned in chapter 4, these offerings are not penalties. The purpose of an offering is not primarily a penalty to appease an angry God so that the offender can avoid a consequence more costly than the offering. Instead, it's a tangible expression of repentance and a desire to reconcile a loving relationship—to restore *shalom*—with the victim and with God. The Bible expresses God's commitment to bringing about restorative justice, the kind of justice that restores loving relationships among people and between Him and humankind.

MERCY AND (RETRIBUTIVE) JUSTICE ARE OPPOSITES

Some Christians feel that mercy and justice are mutually exclusive. One story about Napoleon demonstrates this perspective.

A young man had been arrested for twice stealing from the royal palace. Sentenced to hang, the boy's mother sought mercy from Napoleon on behalf of her son.

Napoleon answered the mother's plea. "This boy has stolen from my palace twice now. He deserves justice, and that justice is death."

"But I don't ask for justice, your highness," the mother said. "I seek mercy."

"He does not deserve mercy," replied Napoleon.

"It would not be mercy if he deserved it!"

Touched by the mother's grief and passion, Napoleon consented and released the boy.

> *Retributive justice is opposite to mercy. The only way to satisfy both is through two opposing acts.*

In this illustration, retributive justice was withheld in order to dispense mercy. Many Christians use such a concept to explain God's forgiveness through Christ. We deserve punishment, and God cannot be just and merciful at the same time without having Christ take our punishment in substitution. As long as we hold on to the retributive definition of justice, mercy and justice will appear to be mutually exclusive attributes of God. We often read in Christian literature that mercy and justice need to be *balanced*, that we need to maintain the *tension* between mercy and justice. God the Father must maintain His perfect (retributive) justice, which is why he must punish all sinners with eternal death. However, God must also maintain His perfect mercy.

Consequently, the only way for God to maintain both is to become Jesus Christ to take the penalty on our behalf. So, God the Son—Jesus Christ—came to save humankind from the punishment imposed by God the Father in order to maintain perfect justice and perfect mercy. God satisfies His need for both justice and mercy by punishing Himself through Christ. A man can go free, unpunished, if he accepts this substitution and becomes a Christian. This is based on one concept: God's (retributive) justice demands that sin be punished. When a person sins by hurting and offending someone (including God), perfect justice is somehow achieved when someone else—in this case, the innocent Son of God—is punished on behalf of the offender.

Retributive justice is opposite to mercy. The only way to satisfy both is through two opposing acts. One is to impose a punishment to achieve retributive justice, and the other is to let an innocent party take the penalty in substitution, thus achieving mercy. Only the sinless eternal God through Christ can counterbalance the punishment of the just eternal God. The cosmic balance between perfect retributive justice and perfect mercy is achieved between God the Father and God the Son.

Now, let us examine how restorative justice and mercy are one and the same.

THE PARENT-FIRST VIEW:
MERCY AND RESTORATIVE JUSTICE ARE COMPLEMENTARY

In restorative justice, mercy *is* justice and justice *is* mercy. Exercising restorative justice to reconcile loving relationships among people and between God and humankind is merciful. When someone sins intentionally or unintentionally, someone else is hurt. When the victim of sin is compensated in accordance with the loss, it is just *and* merciful.

The laws in Exodus 21–22 show us that God stipulates compensation for the victims of offenses. Although culturally the compensations could appear strange to us, we can see that God wants us to restore *shalom* with our neighbors if we have offended them. Through these laws God provides an objective justice we can follow. When I do something wrong and a victim gets hurt, it is unjust and *shalom* is broken. When I follow God's justice by compensating the victim of my wrongdoing for the harm done, justice is served and *shalom* is restored. It is merciful that the victim be compensated for the loss. *Mercy is achieved through exercising restorative justice.*

For example, in Exodus 21:33–34, we read:

If a man uncovers a pit or digs one and fails to cover it and an ox or a donkey falls into it, the owner of the pit must pay for the loss; he must pay its owner, and the dead animal will be his.

It was unintentional, but someone experiences a loss, and the offender must restore the loss. Note that the offender gets to keep the dead animal.

In Exodus 22:1, we read:

If a man steals an ox or a sheep and slaughters it or sells it, he must pay back five head of cattle for the ox and four sheep for the sheep.

Not only is the victim compensated; the thief has to pay back more than what he stole. In this case, although there is a punishment, the intent is not retribution but prevention. It's a deterrent. It is *just and merciful* that the victim who suffers a loss receive restoration of his or her

> *Instead of setting aside retributive justice to exercise mercy, mercy is achieved through exercising restorative justice.*

properties and more. It is also *just and merciful* that the offender pays over and above the loss and, it is hoped, learns not to steal again so that others don't suffer further from this thief. Instead of setting aside retributive justice to exercise mercy, mercy is achieved through exercising restorative justice. When the victim is compensated and the thief learns to steal no more, *shalom* is restored in the community.

This concept isn't restricted to the Old Testament. For example, in Luke 19:1–9, we read about Zacchaeus, a tax collector who repented and gave half his possessions to the poor, paying back four times what he had cheated out of others. Zacchaeus obeyed biblical restorative justice when he decided to follow Jesus.

In Micah 6:6–8, we read:

With what shall I come before the Lord
and bow down before the exalted God?
Shall I come before him with burnt offerings,
with calves a year old?
Will the Lord be pleased with thousands of rams,
with ten thousand rivers of oil?
Shall I offer my firstborn for my transgression,
the fruit of my body for the sin of my soul?
He has showed you, O man, what is good.
And what does the Lord require of you?
To act justly and to love mercy
and to walk humbly with your God.

In the first two verses, Micah was inquiring on behalf of God's people to discover how he could please God. Here is God's answer: "To act justly and to love mercy and to walk humbly with your God." Justice and mercy are twins—to act justly is to love mercy. Justice is mercy only when it's restorative, however, because there's no mercy in retributive justice.

God is perfectly just and perfectly merciful. God gives us laws and commandments to rescue us from the pain of broken relationships we cause through our sins. God is committed to exercising justice because He is merciful. *Retributive* justice points to a stern judge who finds it necessary to punish offenders simply to maintain His standard of justice. *Restorative* justice points to a loving Father who is committed to exercising justice, thus reconciling us to Him and other people to restore relational peace.

THE FORK IN THE ROAD

There are two views of justice—which do you think the Bible teaches? I think the Bible teaches restorative justice, so that when God judges He brings about restoration of shalom between humankind and Himself —our vertical relationship—and among humans—our horizontal relationship. It's the difference between a judge and a parent.

When I shared this message during a Sunday sermon at my church, a mother commented about retributive justice. She said something like this: "It takes a pretty sick mom or dad to find it necessary to punish their children for every wrongdoing just so they can maintain justice or their dignity."

I agree.

So, here we are, at another fork in the road. When we think about biblical justice, do we take the path that leads to an immovable judge administering inflexible retributive justice, or do we take the path that leads to a relentlessly loving parent administering restorative justice to bring about *shalom* among His children and with Himself?

I've shared this with Anglicans, Catholics, and other non-evangelical Christians and never heard a single objection. The only objections come from evangelicals. Although few argue with the line of reasoning in this chapter, the objection usually comes in the form of another "What about…?" question: What about God's wrath and the punishment of sins in the Bible?

We'll turn to this question next.

What About God's Wrath?

SIX

GOD'S ANGER AND HUMAN ATROCITY

"God is angry," the pastor said.

She was the pastor of a church and the wife of a colleague at work. We were talking in the office about recent reports of massacres and rape from a country in Africa. She was expressing how God would feel about the people who committed atrocities in these conflicts. The organization we worked for had many colleagues on the ground serving the poor, often in refugee camps in underdeveloped and war-torn areas. These colleagues sent us firsthand reports of human cruelty: preteen children forced into armed conflicts as soldiers, genocides, powerbrokers using the starvation of civilians as a political tactic, villages uprooted and people murdered to clear the land for natural resource "development" projects such as mining and drilling for oil, and more. These human tragedies were frequent topics of discussion.

It is well known to relief agencies that mass starvation is caused mostly by humans. Droughts often trigger famines, but international relief efforts are normally up to the task of feeding the hungry. Mass starvation is caused by one or more factions in a conflict intentionally depriving people of their access to food.

Such is the case at the time of this writing. The Horn of Africa is facing another massive famine. International relief efforts are in full swing.

> [A]l-Shabab [an Islamist militant group], which continues to control much of southern Somalia, has denied that a famine is taking place and has been blocking humanitarian aid and aid workers. There have also been reports that al-Shabaab is preventing starving Somalis from fleeing to government-controlled areas where aid is more easily accessible.[29]

As al-Shabab exercises its military muscle, thousands of people die of starvation in spite of relief efforts.

THE TRADITIONAL JUDGE-FIRST VIEW

Anger is a natural response when we see outrageous violations of human rights and decency, especially when we hear about people committing murder, acts of terrorism, sexual assault, and child abuse, offenses seemingly much worse than our own sins.

Most would readily acknowledge that none of us is perfect. Indeed, the Bible teaches that all have sinned. But how can I compare my seemingly trivial sins with these atrocities? For example, I tend to exaggerate my vocational accomplishments in job interviews. How can I compare this with the perversion of creating and selling child pornography over the Internet? Overstating expenses or understating income on income tax returns—that surely cannot be as sinful as robbing an old lady of her purse! I hope there is nothing I can dream of doing that is as atrocious as the deeds of those who force preteens, boys and girls who are barely ten years old, to become soldiers or sexual objects.

The truth is that, during quiet reflective moments, when we are honest with ourselves, most of us would admit that we have hurt others through our wrongdoings. Sometimes the memories are so painful that we block them out. At times those memories surface and hit us hard. Other times, when we're hurt by others, especially those we love, we carry those memories for the rest of our lives. Like an old injury, the hurt comes back during tender moments and we relive those hurts as though they happened yesterday. We sin against ourselves, other people, and God.

So, what does God do when he sees us sin? How does God respond when he sees us hurting ourselves, other people, and Him? The response is often what we call "God's wrath." For many, God's wrath results in judgment and punishment in this world and in eternity. Being saved from God's wrath is the reason people need salvation. The Bible does describe God's wrath, but the traditional interpretation is deeply rooted in the narrow definition of retributive justice we have already discussed. Understanding God's wrath and judgment requires that we constantly keep in mind the difference between retributive and restorative justice.

I warn you now that it won't be easy because a retributive God administering inflexible justice has been a "baked-in" premise of our teachings about God, not just for Christians but also for most of the world's people. Many basic Christian doctrines have been developed and taught over the centuries based on the concept of a retributive God. Traditional teachings about God's wrath are also heavily based on the concept of a retributive God.

The previous fork in the road, which differentiated between retributive and restorative justice, is an important paradigm shift for most Christians. Keep that choice in mind as we discuss God's wrath.

LET'S DIG MORE DEEPLY

The Bible teaches that we will face God's wrath sooner or later. We often use the words *wrath* and *anger* interchangeably. Some explain *wrath* as anger in action, or intense anger. An online dictionary returns the following definitions:

> Strong, stern, or fierce anger; deeply resentful indignation; ire; punishment or vengeance as a manifestation of anger; divine retribution for sin; vengeance or punishment as the consequence of anger; intense anger (usually on an epic scale).[30]

Let's review what we've discussed so far about sin and its impact on our relationship with God. For example, the Bible teaches that the loving relationship between God and Adam and Eve ended when they disobeyed God, became afraid of Him, and hid from Him in the Garden of Eden. God didn't terminate the loving relationship; Adam and Eve did, when they hid from God, who came into the Garden seeking their fellowship. Therefore, although God's prediction came true (that Adam and Eve would die when they ate the fruit from the Tree of the Knowledge of Good and Evil), God didn't pronounce and execute the sentence of death. Adam and Eve sinned and then proceeded to turn away from God, hiding from Him. God had warned them by telling them what the consequence would be.

Further, we've noted that God was the primary part of the loving relationship. The Bible says, "We love because [God] first loved us" (1 John 4:19). A relationship connects at least two parties. Both God and humankind participated in this loving relationship. Therefore, if we experienced death in the termination of the loving relationship, God experienced the same death. God is eternal, meaning that His existence doesn't have a beginning or an end. God never dies. We cannot say that we cause God's death, but when humankind sins and causes the death of the loving relationship with God, God experiences fully the grief, loss, hurt, despair, and pain that comes from the death of that relationship.

But we cannot stop here. We need to remember that God is infinite and perfect—He loves infinitely and perfectly. When we spurn God's infinite and perfect love, God's pain is deep, beyond the comprehension of our finite and imperfect minds. Remembering this helps us catch a glimpse of something no mortal can ever come close to fully understanding: the pain of God.

OUR PAIN AND GOD'S PAIN

We experience pain from birth until the day we die. Pain is never welcome. Over our lifetimes we develop ways to avoid and lessen physical and emotional pain. We work hard at it. Often, we reduce our sensitivity and

> *It's ironic that through the process of covering up our sins, we* add *to our sins.*

vulnerability to pain through defensiveness, insulation, and avoidance. We try to prove that we're right even when we know deep inside we're wrong. We avoid people with whom we feel uncomfortable. We try to steer away from painful subjects in our conversations. We strive to reduce our sensitivity to pain.

As much as we loathe pain, the irony is that we cause our own pain. We are imperfect and we do wrong, intentionally and unintentionally. When we sin, we hurt others, God, and ourselves. Although we cause pain, we also try to insulate ourselves from pain. For example, after we've done something wrong and get caught, our natural tendency is to deny it because it's painful to admit our mistakes. Often, the more serious the mistake, the more we deny it.

Furthermore, after we start the process of denial, we work harder and harder to cover up our denial. Every time a layer of denial gets worn out or penetrated, we put on a thicker layer to cover up the previous layer. As each layer becomes more defensive and more inventive, we talk ourselves into believing the denials and fabricate more elaborate "truths" to prove we've been right from the beginning. We sin to try to become righteous, or at least to appear blameless to others. It's ironic that through the process of covering up our sins we *add* to our sins.

The problem with our defensiveness is that we become so self-centered and self-righteous while insulating ourselves from the pain of sin that we stop caring whether we hurt others. We take much more time thinking about how to escape the consequences of our own sin than about the pain we cause others, including the pain we cause God. We tend to focus more on Adam and Eve's pain in their expulsion from Eden than on God's pain. Few theologians and writers discuss how painful it was for God as the perfectly loving parent when His children believed the lies of the serpent instead of His words, disobeyed Him, became afraid of Him, hid from Him, and finally blamed Him for their disobedience.

How many people have written about the pain our Perfect Parent felt in the Garden of Eden? We often talk about the consequences of sin, the judgment of Almighty God, and the loss of our eternal life as though we're the only ones who are hurting. To make it worse, we talk as though our Father is the one who inflicts the penalty and pain, even though

> *Most interpretations focus on the consequences we suffer in Genesis 3 and blame God for cursing us, which causes us to ignore the pain we inflict on God when we sin.*

the Bible text clearly shows that Adam and Eve were the ones who turned away from God, terminating the loving relationship. Most interpretations focus on the consequences we suffer in Genesis 3 and blame God for cursing us, which causes us to ignore the pain we inflict on God when we sin.

THE PARENT-FIRST VIEW

God expresses His anguish over our sins in many ways. One of the most vulnerable expressions of God's pain is found in Hosea, where we read about how God told the prophet Hosea to marry Gomer, an unfaithful woman. In obedience, Hosea married Gomer who bore him three children but repeatedly prostituted herself to others. Amazingly, God told Hosea to take her back. God used this to illustrate His love for Israel in spite of their repeated rebellions against Him.

If we were to look at God as an unfeeling old man, we could gloss over such illustrations of love, anguish, and forgiveness. By remembering God as our loving Father, however, we can appreciate God's vulnerability in desiring a loving relationship with us, not to mention the anguish He suffers when we repeatedly spurn His outreached hand of reconciliation. We shouldn't overlook the intensity of God's pain in our disobedience and rejection of Him.

Try to put aside the image of a stern judge and think of God as a loving parent, then read the following passage:

When Israel was a child, I loved him,
And out of Egypt I called My son.
As they called them,
So they went from them;
They sacrificed to the Baals,
And burned incense to carved images.
I taught Ephraim to walk,
Taking them by their arms;

But they did not know that I healed them.
I drew them with gentle cords,
With bands of love,
And I was to them as those who take the yoke from their neck.
I stooped and fed them....
My people are bent on backsliding from Me.
Though they call to the Most High,
None at all exalt Him.
How can I give you up, Ephraim?
How can I hand you over, Israel?
How can I make you like Admah?
How can I set you like Zeboiim?
My heart churns within Me;
My sympathy is stirred.
I will not execute the fierceness of My anger;
I will not again destroy Ephraim.
For I am God, and not man,
The Holy One in your midst;
And I will not come with terror.
(Hosea 11:1–4, 7–9, NKJV)

Can you see the intense anguish God suffers? How many of us could so vulnerably express our love for another who has repeatedly spurned and despised our love? Instead of thundering as the Almighty God about how disgraceful it was for the nations of Israel and Judah to turn against Him, God took the identity of an abandoned lover, the forsaken victim of an unfaithful spouse, and pleaded for the return of His children.

This vulnerability is also expressed by Jesus. In the parable of the Prodigal Son, we see not only the father who "saw [the son] and was filled with compassion for him; he ran to his son, threw his arms around him and kissed him" (Luke 15:20), but also the father who "went out and pleaded with [the older son]" (Luke 15:28), who was angry with him for welcoming back his brother. It's important for us to see God beyond being an immovable judge. We must pay attention to these passages that show a parent who desires more than anything else a loving relationship with us.

With this as a foundation, let's examine the wrath of God as the Bible describes it.

GOD'S WRATH

Without question, God expresses His wrath toward sin and lawlessness. But what is this *wrath?* Is it the kind of anger that triggers retribution and punishment? Is it the kind of anger that requires the sinners' suffering before the anger can be appeased? Let's see what the Bible teaches.

For the wrath of God is revealed from heaven against all ungodliness and unrighteousness of men, who suppress the truth in unrighteousness, because what may be known of God is manifest in them, for God has shown it to them. For since the creation of the world His invisible attributes are clearly seen, being understood by the things that are made, even His eternal power and Godhead, so that they are without excuse, because, although they knew God, they did not glorify Him as God, nor were thankful, but became futile in their thoughts, and their foolish hearts were darkened. Professing to be wise, they became fools, and changed the glory of the incorruptible God into an image made like corruptible man—and birds and four-footed animals and creeping things. Therefore God also gave them up to uncleanness, in the lusts of their hearts, to dishonor their bodies among themselves, who exchanged the truth of God for the lie, and worshiped and served the creature rather than the Creator, who is blessed forever. Amen. (Romans 1:18–25, NKJV)

What a passage! Without a doubt God responds strongly concerning sin. After reading that passage, no one can say that God is indifferent to sin. God's wrath is clear. It's a strong response to "all the ungodliness and wickedness of human beings" (Romans 1:18, TNIV). But what does this *wrath* mean?

From a biblical basis, in addition to the usual interpretation of anger and indignation, the Greek word for *wrath* also means "movement or

> *"God doesn't get angry because he doesn't get his way. He gets angry because disobedience always results in self-destruction. What kind of father sits by and watches his child hurt himself?"*
> —Max Lucado

agitation of the soul, impulse, desire, any violent emotion, but especially anger."[31] God's wrath shows His deep agitation and emotion about our sins, but that doesn't necessarily imply He must punish sinners with eternal damnation to uphold His holy, just, and righteous attributes. That's an interpretation and an inference, not a direct teaching from the Bible.

Max Lucado, in *Experiencing the Heart of Jesus*, explains God's wrath eloquently:

Many don't understand God's anger because they confuse the wrath of God with the wrath of man. The two have *little* in common. Human anger is typically self-driven and prone to explosions of temper and violent deeds. We get ticked off because we've been overlooked, neglected, or cheated. This is the anger of man. It is not, however, the anger of God.

God doesn't get angry because he doesn't get his way. He gets angry because disobedience always results in self-destruction. What kind of father sits by and watches his child hurt himself? What kind of God would do the same? Do we think he giggles at adultery or snickers at murder? Do you think he looks the other way when we produce television talk shows based on perverse pleasures? Does he shake his head and say, "Humans will be humans"? I don't think so.[32]

As Lucado notes, we cannot compare our anger or wrath with God's wrath. Our feelings are self-centered. We're usually more concerned with how other people make us feel and what they do to us than with how we make others feel and what we do to others. We project our feelings onto God and interpret His wrath as something that requires appeasement. We project our retributive nature to replace God's restorative character; we project our defensiveness to replace God's vulnerable love.

God cares very much about sins because our sins bring death. God is very concerned with our sins. He cares more deeply about our sins than any of us can imagine. But God's response to our sins isn't anger as humans tend to express it—and especially not the kind of anger that triggers a need for retribution or appeasement.

Trevor Seath, my pastor and friend for many years, wrote to me about God's wrath:

> When we celebrate our estrangement from our Creator through a multitude of actions which place ourselves on the throne of our own universe…we elevate that which is our shame. It is like eating vomit. God is offended by sins because they are pathetic and deadly. Actions that celebrate our essential disease are pure foolishness. In sinful actions we are not so much violating a divine code of conduct as we are proudly trumpeting what is most broken and ugly about us. At such wilful perversion, God's stomach turns and His eyes fill with tears. He rants. He raves. It is insanity and He thunders across the universe to return us to a perception of reality—to help us see that our distance from Him is our demise. We are like toddlers dancing in celebration of our freedom in the middle of a busy street. He is like our father who screams and waves and beckons wildly from the curb. Our wilful distance from the Father (which is sin) means that we will die. Celebrating our condition (what we think of as sinful action) only makes the tragedy more unbearable for the God who loves us.

When people hurt us, our instinct—our *human* instinct—is to hurt back, often in the name of justice. We often project our instinct onto God. To a certain extent, we make God in our own image. God definitely responds to our sins with wrath, but God's wrath is different from human anger. When we get angry, we often want to lash out in retribution to hurt others and make them pay. That often results in demands for punishment and appeasement.

WHAT GOD DOES IN HIS WRATH

As we discovered earlier, the biblical laws uphold *restorative* justice, not retributive justice. God's response to sin is *restoration*.

Jesus teaches us in Matthew 5–6, a passage commonly referred to as the Sermon on the Mount, to respond to evil with good, turn the other cheek, and walk an extra mile. Later, in Matthew 18:21–22, Jesus teaches Peter about forgiveness:

> *Then Peter came to Jesus and asked, "Lord, how many times shall I forgive someone who sins against me? Up to seven times?"*
> *Jesus answered, "I tell you, not seven times, but seventy-seven times."*
> (TNIV)

Jesus says nothing about exercising justice *before* we offer forgiveness. Jesus doesn't teach Peter to exact punishment from those who sin against him before forgiving them, so why would we expect God to do the exact opposite? There's no biblical reason for us to expect God to insist on punishing every sin and every sinner both in this life and through eternity.

Therefore, it makes sense to consider carefully and biblically this terrifying thing called "the wrath of God." It makes sense to back off our human perspective of anger and think about what the Bible really teaches. In our study of Genesis 3, we learned about God's reason for disallowing access to the tree of life, which would have enabled humans to live forever physically. The same principle applies to understanding God's wrath. It isn't anger that demands punishment or vengeance, but a firm commitment from God to limit evil and prevent us from imposing further harm.

God does take action against sin. In doing so, He expresses His wrath not as an angry judge but as a loving parent who is committed to the good of all humans. In expressing this wrath, He doesn't exclude His mercy. In fact, it is mercy that motivates God to contain and destroy evil and injustice. Through His wrath God helps us see the dire consequences of our sin so we can return to Him in repentance.

Reread the Romans passage with the backdrop of a loving parent trying to contain and destroy evil and injustice. This time remember our lesson in God's restorative justice. Remember that the Bible teaches about a God who is committed to restoring *shalom*—relational peace—between humankind and Himself and among humans. Remember that God doesn't express anger the way humans do. Remember that God is committed to helping us see our errors so we'll turn to Him for help and healing.

Set aside the image of a stern judge. Think of God as humankind's deeply hurting and loving parent, who watches all that goes on in this world: genocide, child molestation, spousal abuse, murder, lying, cheating, materialism, power struggles, war, terrorism, and numerous other sins. Being omniscient, God knows very well how sinful humankind is. He knows each of us is capable of unmentionable sins under certain combinations of circumstances, cultural upbringings, and pressures. But He is committed to *restoration*, not retribution.

As a loving parent, God is more determined to rescue us from this endless cycle of slavery to sin than He is to punish us for the sake of upholding His own attributes. He does punish and discipline, but the purpose is to express His love—to bring about what's best for us. God is all-sufficient; there's no need for Him to do anything to us for Himself.

I don't want you to miss this last point. It's very important. Does God need to do anything *to us* so as to uphold *His* perfection? Is God damaged in any measure if He doesn't do something *to us*? Where in the Bible do we learn that God has to do something *to us* so that he can maintain the perfection of His attributes?

The Bible clearly teaches what God does to help His children. The definitive teaching summarizing the expression of God's wrath is contained in Hebrews 12:1–11:

> *Therefore, since we are surrounded by such a great cloud of witnesses, let us throw off everything that hinders and the sin that so easily entangles. And let us run with perseverance the race marked out for us, fixing our eyes on Jesus, the pioneer and perfecter of faith. For the joy set before him he endured the cross, scorning its shame, and sat down at the right hand of the throne of God. Consider him who*

endured such opposition from sinners, so that you will not grow weary and lose heart.

In your struggle against sin, you have not yet resisted to the point of shedding your blood. And have you completely forgotten this word of encouragement that addresses you as children? It says,

"My son, do not make light of the Lord's discipline, and do not lose heart when he rebukes you, because the Lord disciplines those he loves, and he chastens everyone he accepts as his child."

Endure hardship as discipline; God is treating you as his children. For what children are not disciplined by their father? If you are not disciplined—and everyone undergoes discipline—then you are not legitimate children at all. Moreover, we have all had parents who disciplined us and we respected them for it. How much more should we submit to the Father of spirits and live! Our parents disciplined us for a little while as they thought best; but God disciplines us for our good, that we may share in his holiness.

No discipline seems pleasant at the time, but painful. Later on, however, it produces a harvest of righteousness and peace for those who have been trained by it. (TNIV)

Therefore, to anyone who asks whether God punishes, the answer is "Yes." When God punishes, however, it's in the spirit of disciplining for the purpose of training and restoration. When God punishes, it's for our betterment. God doesn't need to do anything to us to satisfy Himself, or any of His attributes, in any way.

When I express the opinion that God isn't an immovable judge administering inflexible (retributive) justice through punishment to all sinners for eternity, many jump to the conclusion that I advocate a God who never punishes. There's a lot of distance between a God who must punish every sin with eternal punishment and a God who never punishes. I find it necessary to clarify that I don't advocate a God who looks the other way when it comes to sin. God does punish, but He punishes for our good. The reason isn't retribution. God's punishments are instructive and restorative for us.

To understand God's wrath, we need to remember that the Bible clearly teaches that God is for us all the way. In Romans 8:28–32, we see that God would do anything for us, including giving up His own son. Even when He disciplines us, God is for us. He does it for our good. I don't know where in the Bible we get the idea that God deems it necessary to do anything *against* us to uphold His own attributes.

So, does God need to do anything to His children to uphold His perfection? No. Rather, God's response to our sin is, "Oh no! What are you doing? You foolish children…see how you're hurting yourselves! See how you're hurting one another! See how you're hurting Me! Stop it! Turn back to Me and My ways of love and compassion. If you insist on hurting yourselves, others, and Me, and keep on refusing to return to Me, I'll let you taste your own medicine so you'll discover the devastation of your sinful ways." That's what God's wrath means: a gut-wrenching "Oh no!" that demonstrates the depths of His anguish, the tenderness of His vulnerability, and His determination to correct and restore us.

That is God's wrath.

GOD'S FOR US, NOT FOR HIMSELF

God's response to sin is wrathful, but His wrath isn't the kind of human anger that prompts Him to punish for the sake of punishing or to uphold His own perfection. This doesn't mean God isn't holy; neither does it mean God doesn't desire righteousness and justice for His creation, now and for eternity. Our sins offend God's righteousness and justice, and He takes action to restore righteousness and justice. But biblical righteousness and justice are different from our sense of righteousness and justice. We feel the need to prove we're perfect and right. God has nothing to prove. We need revenge. God doesn't need to avenge Himself. We project our needs onto the image of God and, in the process, interpret God's wrath as something God never intends it to be.

God's righteousness is expressed well in Micah 6:6–8, which we discussed in chapter 5. God's justice and mercy are one and the same. God's restorative justice is expressed through mercy. When we understand God's wrath in the context of restorative justice, we can see God's mercy even in His wrath. God's wrath is an expression of His anguish at the harm our sins impose on ourselves and our relationship with Him. His punishment is what He does to correct and restore. The Bible teaches that God's wrath is all about God acting *for our own good.*

After my wife read the first draft of this chapter, she commented that it was intense. I agree. The wrath of God is, indeed, intense. Wrath is a deep and intense agitation of the soul. God is intensely agitated about sin, and the depth of His agitation isn't caused by humans offending His dignity or perfection; the depth of His agitation shows His relentless love for us. It shows us how passionately God wants us to live in *shalom* with Him, among ourselves, and with His creation. God's wrath shows His uncompromising commitment and actions to limit evil and bring about reconciliation and restoration of *shalom.*

God would do anything to bring an end to our sin and enable us to reconcile with Him. And that's exactly what Jesus talks about in John 3:16–17:

For God so loved the world that he gave his one and only Son, that whoever believes in him shall not perish but have eternal life. For God did not send his Son into the world to condemn the world, but to save the world through him.

This passage is an unswerving commitment for restoration at infinite cost to Himself. When we repeatedly spurn God's plan for reconciliation and restoration, God powerfully expresses His commitment to contain and destroy our sin, bringing about restoration through His wrath in action.

When God acts on His wrath, He does it for us, not for Himself.

THE FORK IN THE ROAD

This concept of the wrath of God is likely very different from what you've been taught. I hope you take the time to read this and other Bible passages about God's wrath in the context of a deeply concerned parent doing everything possible other than turning us into robots or slaves without free will.[33] Keep asking yourself the key question I mentioned earlier: does God have to do anything to us to uphold His own dignity or perfection?

If your answer is "Yes," you'll be steered toward seeing God as an immovable judge administering inflexible retributive justice and seeing wrath as God's expression of intense anger to punish us for our offenses.

If your answer is "No," I hope you accept the view that God is a relentlessly loving parent administering restorative justice, seeing wrath as God's uncompromising commitment to limiting evil and bringing about reconciliation and restoration.

If your answer is "I don't know," I hope you'll pursue your own study with an open mind.

The next question people often ask is, "What about the punishments I read about in the Bible, both in the Old Testament and the New Testament?" That's where we'll turn next.

What About God's Punishment for Sin?

SEVEN

THE TRADITIONAL JUDGE-FIRST VIEW

All Bible authors except Luke were Jewish. Christian converts after the first century, however, were predominantly Gentiles with Greek and Roman cultural backgrounds. Modern translators are mostly from the Western culture. As we discussed earlier, most Greco-Roman Christians came from cultures accustomed to retributive justice.[34] Therefore, it doesn't come as a surprise that many theologians and translators interpreted the original Hebrew and Greek texts with a retributive bias.

This interpretation has resulted in a coherent but biased framework of a judge-first view of God. The retributive justice mindset has guided our interpretation of scripture and the concepts of punishment and justice not only in Christians, but also in the Western world in general. This mindset doesn't harmonize well with the Hebrew concept of justice, which is based on the Hebrew Bible, the Old Testament.

THE EMPHASIS ON PUNISHMENT
AND PENALTY IN SOME TRANSLATIONS

To understand the impact of how a framework affects general interpretation, I conducted a search on terms related to punishment in three translations of the Bible—the New Living Translation (NLT), the English Standard Version (ESV), and the New King James Version (NKJV). The following table shows the frequency of these words' use:

Words/Versions	NLT		ESV		NKJV	
Old/New Testament	OT	NT	OT	NT	OT	NT
Punish	125	12	51	5	46	1
Punishes	6	1	0	0	2	0
Punished	59	13	9	3	18	3
Punishment(s)	65	14	49	8	38	5
Penalty	16	6	3	3	2	0
Penalties	2	0	0	0	0	0
Sub Totals	**273**	**46**	**112**	**19**	**106**	**9**
Totals	**319**		**131**		**115**	

Since the NKJV uses the *p* words the least, at 115 times, we use it as our baseline. The NLT, a paraphrase translation that's more interpretive than literal, uses the *p* words 319 times, 177 percent more often than the NKJV. The ESV, a relatively literal translation, uses them 131 times, 14 percent more than the NKJV. A cursory comparison shows that the NKJV and ESV translators preferred words such as *chastise, discipline, judge,* and *correct* over the *p* words favored by the NLT translators.

The *p* words express a more retributive framework than do the less severe words. Although some passages refer to God's action toward humans and others refer to relations among humans, this usage demonstrates how a particular framework could have guided the translators to use one particular group of words more or less frequently—rightly or wrongly. Clearly, the more literal translations (such as the ESV and NKJV) are more conservative in projecting a punishing God than the NLT, a paraphrase that relies more on the translators' interpretations of the same words in the original languages.[35]

When Jesus spoke about justice in the Gospels, and when Paul wrote about justice in his epistles, their scriptural basis was the Hebrew scripture, the only scripture available at the time. The Hebrew concept of justice is predominantly restorative.[36] Therefore, when it is biblically sound, we should interpret punishment in the restorative justice framework instead of the retributive justice framework. It is in this tone that we proceed.

LET'S DIG MORE DEEPLY

> We should interpret punishment in the restorative justice framework instead of the retributive justice framework.

Consistent with the intent and scope of this book, we'll focus on some representative punishments that are restorative and others that appear to be punitive. I seek to show that there are biblically sound restorative interpretations *if we consider the parent-first framework as context.*

Different kinds of punishments are depicted in the Bible. For example, there are punishments imposed by rulers to keep human laws. In this chapter we'll focus on just two kinds of punishment: divine punishments and church punishments.

EXAMPLES OF DIVINE PUNISHMENTS

Divine punishment is a commonly accepted concept. It isn't restricted to Christian beliefs. For example, after any major tragedy whether manmade or natural, talk of divine punishment abounds. This happened after events such as the 9/11 terrorist act on the World Trade Towers, the 2004 Indonesian tsunami, the 2005 Katrina hurricane, the 2008 Haitian earthquake, and the 2011 Japanese earthquake and tsunami. The media invariably publish comments from political and religious leaders, Christians and otherwise, saying that these tragedies are divine punishments on greed, pride, and immorality. But is this the God that the Bible teaches us about?

If we accept the concept that God's wrath is His commitment to eliminate and contain evil and injustice and to restore *shalom*, then punishments in the Bible represent God's actions as a consequence of His wrath. Instead of looking at punishments in the Bible from the perspective of retribution or vengeance or of God doing anything *to us* to satisfy His need to uphold His own perfection, we seek biblical grounds to interpret God's punishments as His actions to eliminate and contain evil and injustice.

For example, recall our discussion about Adam and Eve's expulsion from Eden, which most have traditionally interpreted as God's judgment (or punishment) for disobedience. We showed that the reason for the expulsion was God's action to contain evil and injustice by removing access to physical eternal life.[37] The love relationship among the first humans and God was poisoned by sin. In addition to turning from God, Adam and Eve expressed no repentance. Instead, Adam blamed Eve and God, and Eve blamed the serpent. There was no confession. God's expulsion of Adam and Eve from Eden was an act of kindness to limit their physical lifespan, thus preventing them from hurting themselves forever. In the meantime, God carries out His plan for eternal redemption and reconciliation through Christ.

Another example I'm often asked about is the punishment of Achan and his family after the conquest of Jericho, in Joshua 7. The Israelites irrevocably committed to God all the spoils of war in the conquest of Jericho. Achan was unfaithful to this commitment and kept some of them for himself. At the next campaign at Ai, the Israelites were defeated by a much weaker enemy. God revealed to Joshua that God wasn't on the Israelites' side in this campaign because of their lack of devotion. When it was shown that Achan was the culprit, he confessed. As a result Achan and "all that he [had]" were stoned and burned.

It's generally assumed that the punishment was extended to Achan's wife and children, but according to some commentaries, there's room for uncertainty. It's possible that Achan and his possessions perished, but not his family members. His family was brought as witnesses to the valley where he was stoned, not necessarily to be executed themselves. But whether Achan alone or his family perished, it was severe punishment.

Those who ask about Achan also tend to ask about another event concerning devotion and death in the New Testament: Ananias and Sapphira in Acts 5:1–11. The interpretations of these two events are similar, and I'll discuss them together.

Acts 4:33–37 tells us about the boldness, unity, and devotion of the early church:

> *With great power the apostles continued to testify to the resurrection of the Lord Jesus, and much grace was upon them all. There were no needy persons among them. For from time to time those who owned lands or houses sold them, brought the money from the sales and put it at the apostles' feet, and it was distributed to anyone as he had need. Joseph, a Levite from Cyprus, whom the apostles called Barnabas (which means Son of Encouragement), sold a field he owned and brought the money and put it at the apostles' feet.*

In Acts 5:1–15, we read about Ananias and Sapphira, who also sold a piece of property. Instead of coming forward with the full proceeds of the sale, they kept back part of the money for themselves. When asked about it, Ananias lied and claimed that he had brought all the proceeds. Peter reprimanded him and Ananias "fell down and died" (Acts 5:5). About three hours later, Sapphira told the same lie. She also fell down at Peter's feet and died.

In both Joshua 7 and Acts 5, the offenders died. There was no chance for restoration for them *in this life*. It's easy to interpret that they died because they offended God. Indeed, Peter told Ananias and Sapphira that they had lied not just to humans but also to God. So, how are we to interpret this in the context of the view that God is a relentlessly loving parent administering restorative justice, not an immovable judge administering inflexible retributive justice?

In Joshua 7:26, we read that "the Lord turned from His fierce anger." In other words, He turned from His wrath. This is where we need to remember the meaning of *wrath*. If we accept that the wrath of God is God's firm commitment to limit sin and destroy injustice, we understand that *God turned from His wrath not because He was appeased but because His purpose was to warn the Israelites against further disobedience.*

This event happened at the start of the conquest of the Promised Land. God used this stern response to teach the Israelites the seriousness of disobedience and greed. God wanted the community to understand its need to rely on God through obedience and its need to remain strong through unity. If disobedience and greed weren't strongly discouraged at the beginning of the conquest, sin would have spread like uncontrolled cancer across the whole community. People would have looked more to their own selfish interests instead of following the leadership of God through Joshua for the good of the whole community. Without dependence on God and unity among the people, the conquest of the Promised Land would have been impossible.

We can seek to understand the deaths of Ananias and Sapphira in Acts 5 in the same vein.

When I was taking a course in church history at seminary, I asked the professor, "There was no such thing as a New Testament and no formal doctrine about Christianity in the first few centuries, so how did the church manage to explode across the Mediterranean, apart and distinct from the Jewish and Greco-Roman cultures and in the face of persecution from the Romans and opposition from the Jews?" The professor smiled and gave me a simple answer: "By the way they lived."

There was no social welfare, no relief agencies, no unemployment insurance, no healthcare plans, and no orphanages. People of all ages who fell into misfortune without support from families, the community, or friends simply perished. Inspired by the teachings of Jesus Christ, guided by manuscripts written by the apostles and Luke, and empowered by the Holy Spirit, a revolutionary community emerged. The early Christian community practiced love and compassion. It took care of everyone in need out of sacrificial sharing from those who had the ability and wealth. They were united in their devotion to God and love for one another. People flocked to the community, attracted by the loving way Christians lived. As a result Christianity exploded in spite of severe persecution from ruling authorities and opposition from the Jews.

In contrast, Ananias and Sapphira decided to lie about their giving. We can interpret that God was angry with Ananias and Sapphira because their deceit amounted to lying to both the church and the Holy Spirit (Acts 5:3, 9). It is reasonable, however, to interpret this drastic disciplinary action in the context of the good of the whole church.

In Acts 5:5 and 5:11, we read that great fear seized the whole church and everyone who heard about these events. God taught the church the importance of relating to one another not only in generosity but especially in integrity and honesty. God's disciplinary action was drastic, but it would be difficult to imagine how Christianity could have swept through the Mediterranean in just a few generations if hypocrisy and dishonesty had been allowed to fester unchecked, contaminating the community of love and devotion to God and people.

In both cases, God acted to preserve the purity and devotion of communities through drastic action. Selfishness, dishonesty, and hypocrisy were limited and discouraged right at the beginning so that God's people could carry out His grand plan of reconciliation and restoration. We see God's wrath in action not simply to protect His own perfection or to express His indignation, but to express His firm commitment to limit evil and promote *shalom* through drastic actions.

We need to discuss the lack of opportunity for the earthly restoration of Achan, Ananias, and Sapphira. It may seem that their deaths were overly harsh. However, the Bible teaches that the end of one's life on earth isn't the ultimate end. We'll discuss the topic of our eternal destinies later in the book, but we don't have to assume that none of them live in God's eternal presence. We're unaware of their faith in God before the immediate events leading to their deaths; we know only that they sinned. We also know that we've all sinned, often more seriously than what Achan, Ananias, and Sapphira did. It's true they died at the hand of God as a result of their earthly sins, but we don't know their eternal destinies. We cannot assume that they haven't been reconciled and restored. We can trust that God treats them with as much compassion and restorative justice as we ourselves can hope and expect in accordance with God's relentless parental love.

Next, we turn to punishments within the church.

CHURCH PUNISHMENTS

Another favorite "What about…?" question is based on 1 Corinthians 5:1–6 and 1 Timothy 1:19–20. In the first case, Paul writes about a Christian who "has his father's wife" (1 Corinthians 5:1).[38] In the second case, two persons suffered "shipwreck" with respect to their faith. In both cases Paul advises that the offenders be handed over to Satan. In 1 Corinthians 5:5, Paul adds that the purpose is the destruction of flesh "so that the sinful nature may be destroyed and his spirit saved on the day of the Lord."

There's no consensus from commentaries regarding what "handed over to Satan" means, although many assume it means excommunication from the church. Adam Clarke notes that there were no equivalent Jewish writings at the time to indicate Paul was giving instructions based on Jewish traditions.[39] Further, there also isn't any consensus regarding the meaning of "destruction of the flesh." In extreme cases it could mean that offenders could be killed by Satan, but Paul probably didn't mean that. The TNIV and NIV substitute the term *sinful nature* in place of *flesh* or *body*. In this case we can interpret that the church members were to be left to their own devices if they insisted on living apart from the faith. Their dominance by evil would bring them so low that they'd recognize the futility and harm that comes from living in accordance with their sinful nature (the flesh), abandon their sinful pursuits, and return to their faith.

Indeed, this is exactly what happens in 2 Corinthians 2:5–11, when Paul urges the same church to welcome back a repentant brother. Although we can't be certain it's the same person as in 1 Corinthians 5, the spirit of welcoming back a brother who has suffered the folly of his sins applies just the same.

As I type this, my wife and I are going through a fresh application of this lesson. We've become quite close to a friend from our church, David (not his real name), who has had multiple bouts of drug addiction and jail sentences since his teen years. Several years ago he became a Christian when he was in jail. He relapsed several times, however, and ended up in jail as a repeat offender. Most recently, he's managed to stay clean for two years.

David had an amazing ability to remember Bible texts and was able to quote passages from memory. He was also quite eloquent in verbalizing his understanding of the Bible. He attended our church regularly and had aspirations of going to seminary to become a pastor. We agreed that with proper training and discipline, he had the potential for full-time Christian work.

One night David called me for help. He claimed his car had broken down in a nearby town. He needed a relatively long-distance tow but had no cash or credit card. He asked me to wire him $125 to pay for the tow truck. It cost me another $35 in fees to send the money through Western Union, but I did it. We found out the next day that he had relapsed. He came to visit a few days afterward, claiming that it had just been a 48-hour blip and that he was back to drug-free living. Although we were skeptical, we didn't challenge him and promised to support him.

Two days later we learned that he was out on the street, back on drugs. His heartbroken girlfriend combed the streets and found him. She took him to breakfast and tried to convince him to check into a nearby detox center. After breakfast David excused himself to go to the bathroom. After an hour of anxious waiting, his girlfriend asked a passerby to check the men's washroom and found that he had escaped through a bathroom window. At the time of this writing, he's wanted by the police for theft and hasn't been seen or heard from for two weeks. He has probably left town.

The best thing for David is to be caught by the police and thrown into jail again, where he can restart his life from the bottom. There would be no use for anyone to seek him out to bring him back into the fold. He has to willingly return, just like the prodigal son to his father. Not even his girlfriend's tearful pleas could convince him to submit to God's love and will.

David knows the Bible well; he can preach very well from it. He knowingly and wilfully discarded what he previously acknowledged to be the truth and returned to his addiction. This is likely what Paul refers to in 1 Timothy 1:19–20 about Christians "shipwrecking" their faith. David's determination to do things his own way has left us no choice but to "hand him over to Satan," with the hope that his flesh, i.e. sinful addiction and self-centered nature, may be destroyed so that he returns to faith.[40]

THE PARENT-FIRST VIEW

Let's review. Except for extreme cases—such as the deaths of Achan, Ananias, and Sapphira, where there was no recourse on earth for the offenders—I prefer to view all biblical punishments, whether coming directly from God or through His church, as discipline and correction.

This interpretation is consistent with the other forks in the road in terms of our understanding of a parent-first or judge-first God.

In chapter 2 we saw God pronouncing a warning instead of a judgment. In chapter 3 we came to view the expulsion from Eden as an act of kindness instead of punishment. In chapter 4 we saw the Levitical laws as offerings for reconciliation instead of penalties for offenses. In chapter 5 we saw that God's justice is more restorative than retributive. In chapter 6 we viewed God's wrath as His fierce commitment to limit and destroy sin and injustice instead of an angry expression of His displeasure.

> *God's anger and wrath represent His determination to limit and destroy sin and injustice, and His punishments are His anger and wrath in action.*

The diagram opposite summarizes the forks in the road we've encountered so far.

In this chapter we can see that biblical punishments are forms of discipline intended for our own good, not something God does to us in vengeance or to uphold the perfection of His attributes. This aligns well with Hebrews 12:1–11.

> *Our parents disciplined us for a little while as they thought best; but God disciplines us* for our good, *that we may share in his holiness. No discipline seems pleasant at the time, but painful. Later on, however, it produces a harvest of righteousness and peace for those who have been trained by it.* (Hebrews 12:10–11, TNIV, emphasis added.)

We need to remind ourselves that God's anger and wrath aren't the same as ours. God's anger and wrath represent His determination to limit and destroy sin and injustice, and His punishments are His anger and wrath in action. He punishes for our good, not for His own good. Even when the punishment seems severe, leaving no room for repentance or restoration for the offender in this life, the punishment serves a greater purpose for the good of the community. Further, there is no biblical evidence that those who perish as a result of God's earthly punishment perish for eternity; there may be hope for them in eternity.

THE FORK IN THE ROAD

We face another choice. We can interpret God's punishments as something God does *to* us to appease Himself as judge, or we can interpret God's punishments as something God does *for our good* as parent.

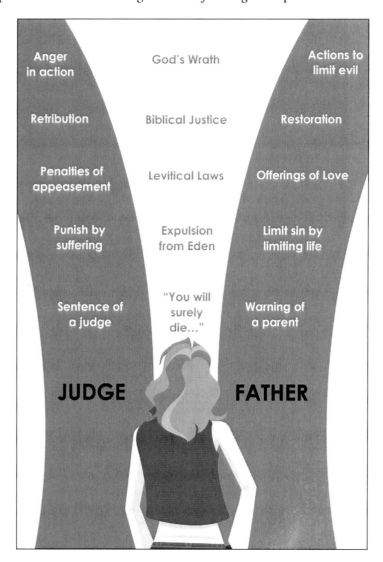

What's your choice?

The follow-up "What about...?" questions usually refer to God's judgment at the end times. In the next chapter, I will address some of them.

What About "All Have Sinned" and "The Wages of Sin"?

EIGHT

JOHN THE EVANGELIST AND THE ROMAN ROAD

One Sunday afternoon I got a call from Judy, a friend from our church. Judy had been watering the church flowerbeds when she noticed a man hanging around. She asked him whether she could help. The man introduced himself as John and told her he wanted to talk to someone about God, so she called me.

It turned out John was going through a difficult time with relationships and was seeking God's guidance. He had a church background but hadn't been cultivating his relationship with God or going to church. My wife and I met John at church and brought him to our home. After talking with us, John recommitted his life to faith in Christ.

John and his colleagues worked as technicians at Toronto's Pearson International Airport readying planes between flights. The work usually involved long waits between landings and frenzied action when the planes were at the gates. During quieter shifts the waits were especially boring and the technicians loitered in the waiting room, chatting.

After renewing his faith in Christ, John made good use of "The Roman Road" to share his faith with his bored teammates.

THE TRADITIONAL JUDGE-FIRST VIEW

The Roman Road is a popular and simple way for Christians to share their faith. It consists of three verses from Romans:

> *For all have sinned and fall short of the glory of God.* (Romans 3:23)
> *For the wages of sin is death, but the gift of God is eternal life in Christ Jesus our Lord.* (Romans 6:23)
> *That if you confess with your mouth, "Jesus is Lord," and believe in your heart that God raised him from the dead, you will be saved.* (Romans 10:9)

Here's the explanation. In Romans 3:23, God's glory is the expression of His perfect character. None of us is perfect because no one can claim to be perfect like God. We have all missed the mark of God's perfection. That's what sin means: missing the mark.

Romans 6:23 tells us that God cannot accept sin in His presence. Sinners, therefore, cannot enjoy eternal life with God. Life in hell without God is what death means. But God doesn't want us to suffer in hell, so he provided us with the gift of salvation through Christ Jesus.

Romans 10:9 tells us clearly what it takes to receive this wonderful gift of salvation. We declare with our mouths that Jesus is Lord and believe that he has risen from the dead. By doing so we are saved from spiritual death in hell.

John had these verses printed on a slip of paper. He showed them to his airport colleagues and explained to them this way of salvation. Then he told them that by praying a simple sinner's prayer, they could become Christians. Many of them prayed to receive Jesus into their lives.

LET'S DIG MORE DEEPLY

We applauded John's evangelistic zeal. I envied his openness and courage in sharing his faith so faithfully and simply. In the back of my mind, however, was the same question that had started the discovery process for this book. It's the same question I asked about the Kidz Camp children: what about those who have never heard? It's the same barcode

> *When we try to prove to our unchurched friends their need for God, we often minimize the goodness in others who aren't Christians… We end up representing a God who focuses on sin but not on the good that's in people.*

Christianity problem we discussed in chapter 1. Those who have sincerely prayed the sinner's prayer receive a barcode that God scans when they die and they go to heaven, regardless of their good and bad deeds. Those who haven't prayed don't get the barcode and they go to hell, regardless of their deeds.

For those without the barcode, even the tiniest infraction makes them deserving of God's eternal punishment. It seems that no matter how much good one performs, God couldn't care less if it isn't done in the name of Christ as a Christian. Many of my evangelical friends would pull out verses such as Isaiah 64:6 to "prove" that God treats our good deeds like filthy rags.[41] That's just the way it is if we don't accept the penalty Christ paid on the cross.

The following joke sadly illustrates this mindset more acutely than most proponents of the viewpoint would like to admit:

An elderly lady was well known for her faith and for her boldness in talking about it. She would stand on her front porch and shout "PRAISE THE LORD!"

Next door to her lived an atheist who would get so angry at her proclamations he would shout, "There ain't no Lord!!"

Hard times set in on the elderly lady, and she prayed for God to send her some assistance. She stood on her porch and shouted, "PRAISE THE LORD. GOD I NEED FOOD!! I AM HAVING A HARD TIME. PLEASE LORD, SEND ME SOME GROCERIES!!"

The next morning the lady went out on her porch and noted a large bag of groceries and shouted, "PRAISE THE LORD."

The neighbor jumped from behind a bush and said, "Aha! I told you there was no Lord. I bought those groceries, God didn't."

The lady started jumping up and down and clapping her hands

and said, "PRAISE THE LORD. He not only sent me groceries, but He made the devil pay for them. Praise the Lord!"[42]

When we try to prove to our unchurched friends their need for God, we often minimize the goodness in others who aren't Christians in order to help them see how their good deeds never live up to God's perfection. In the process, we often achieve the opposite of what we intend. We end up representing a God who focuses on sin but not on the good that's in people.

A SEEMINGLY LOGICAL CHOICE

God appears to be a strict judge as the Father but a forgiving Savior in Christ as the Son. This doesn't make sense to a lot of people.

The Roman Road follows a logical and understandable line of reasoning in explaining why we need to turn to Jesus Christ. This reasoning forms a framework to explain Jesus' sacrifice and the penalties of sin, especially from a human perspective.

We all have a sense of justice. Punishing an offense simply makes sense to us. Letting a criminal go free without consequence doesn't fit our mindset. On the other hand, we've all heard of heroes and heroines who sacrificed themselves for the good of others, and that's exactly what God does through Christ: Jesus gave His life so we could have life. He took the penalty of sin on our behalf. In other words, He paid for our sin.

So, God became man in Jesus Christ and took the penalty on our behalf so that God could, on the one hand, uphold the attribute of justice that requires sin be punished and, on the other hand, bring relief to those who would receive by faith Jesus Christ's sacrifice as substitution for their due penalty. Those who accept the substitution can say to God, "I believe Christ has taken my penalty. You don't need to punish me anymore. Thank you for your gracious forgiveness through Christ." According to this doctrine, God has the basis to forgive sinners because retributive justice has been satisfied through the punishment Jesus Christ received.

A SCHIZOPHRENIC GOD?

Although there were nagging doubts in the back of my mind, this choice was the only way I could explain the "good news." I used this line of logic to convince friends to become Christians, and I'm very glad they did. But as we have discussed, the origin of death is sinners, not God. Adam and Eve turned away from their loving relationship with God in Eden. God did *not* turn away and introduce death. Adam and Eve brought death into creation. The source of the penalty of sin is humankind.

Many are convinced they received Christ along the Roman Road, but many more have questions about it. Responses vary, but these questions tend to revolve around the issue that God appears to be a strict judge as the Father but a forgiving Savior in Christ as the Son. This doesn't make sense to a lot of people. How can God the Father be the immovable judge administering inflexible retributive justice while also being the loving Jesus Christ, who offered Himself to gain forgiveness for humankind?

As a result, I've gotten responses such as:

• You mean God the Son died to save us from God the Father?
• So, God became a human and punished Himself according to His own rules so that He could forgive us?
• This seems more like schizophrenia than justice and love to me, don't you think?
• I didn't ask to be born, you know. How can I trust a God who lets me be born imperfect and then punishes me when He knows I can't help but be imperfect?

Over the years I've heard these objections from those with whom I've shared my faith. I often speculated that their sins prevented them from following such a logical argument, then moved on to my next target of evangelism.

In hindsight, perhaps their sin issues weren't the problem. It was difficult for people to understand my view of God because many find the concept difficult; it seems to set God the Father as a separate person, having a different character from Jesus the Son. God the Father is therefore an immovable judge administering inflexible justice, and Jesus

87

the Son is the gentle and humble Lamb of God who took on our behalf the penalty the judge administered.

In their book, *Recovering the Scandal of the Cross*, authors Joel Green and Mark Baker note:

> Such an understanding…gives rise to such bizarre views as the question, "So Jesus came to save us from God?"—a view that has far more credence in popular views of the atonement than we might want to admit.[43]

Some call it a schizophrenic view of God. Although God relates to us through the Father, the Son, and the Holy Spirit, He also relates to us as three different persons *with totally different, even opposite, characters.*

THE PARENT-FIRST VIEW

Many people, whether Christian or otherwise, feel a level of discomfort imagining God as the Father who insists on punishing sinners just to uphold the perfection of His own attributes. Further, many Christians claim that the punishment is the termination of the loving parent-child relationship *for eternity.* Not only that, but it applies equally to the most trivial white lie or mass murder. Most people aren't treated this way by their parents, and neither do they treat their own children in such a manner. Parents do discipline their children, and the discipline is unpleasant. However, few loving parents find it necessary to respond to their children's sins, no matter how minor or severe, by withdrawing their loving presence—and not just for a while but forever! It would indeed be difficult for us to understand God the Father who both loves infinitely *and* finds it necessary to separate every human from Him for eternity as a penalty for every sin, whether it's a white lie or mass murder.

Proponents of the view of God as an immovable judge administering inflexible retributive justice would point out that we cannot project our human love and sympathy onto God, who is holy, righteous, and just. I used to accept that argument. Indeed, who am I to say how God should uphold His attributes? However, we can apply the same argument both ways. What if God decides, out of His sovereign prerogative, to forgive all sinners simply because he loves every member of the human race? For those who find that argument difficult to believe, is it possible they are projecting their sense of retributive justice and need for revenge onto God, who is perfectly loving and forgiving?

If one begins with the premise that God must do this and not do that, we can apply this logic in opposite ways and arrive at opposite conclusions. We can say that it is necessary for God to punish all sins out of the perfection of His justice. We can also say that it is necessary for God to forgive all sins out of the perfection of His compassion. The bottom line is that we should be very reluctant to decide on behalf of God what He must and must not do.

Without question, the Bible teaches that God judges and punishes sin. God does speak and act in accordance with His righteousness and justice. The Bible teaches that God restores righteousness and justice through judgment, disciplinary action, and punishment. If we choose to believe that God primarily administers *retributive* justice, we can interpret the wages of sin as God-imposed death on every human. However, I hope you've seen enough biblical support for the view that God isn't the originator of the wages of sin. Sinners—that is, all of us—are the originators. The death that all sinners experience isn't God's judgment but the natural consequence of sin.

There's nothing wrong with the Roman Road. Instead there's something wrong in the way we traditionally interpret it by blaming God for the wages of sin. We are sources of the wages of sin. The Roman Road shows us that Jesus is our hope in conquering the consequences of sin, not a formula to escape eternal punishment from an unyielding judge.

THE FORK IN THE ROAD

We're at another fork in the road to the judge-first God or the parent-first God. One way is based on the view that God is an immovable judge administering inflexible retributive justice who imposes the wages of sin on all humankind. The other choice is based on the view that God is a relentlessly loving parent administering restorative justice who gives totally of Himself through Christ to save us from the wages of sin, which we ourselves cause. One path leads you to relate more closely to God as your judge. The other choice leads you to relate more closely to God as your parent.

It's your choice.

What About Final Judgement in Hebrews 9:27?

THE CASE FOR BEING AGNOSTIC

The most talked-about book among our Christian friends during the summer of 2011 was *Love Wins: A Book About Heaven, Hell, and the Fate of Every Person Who Ever Lived*, by Rob Bell. Actually, it was almost universally condemned by our friends. Some call Bell a heretic. This book's Amazon.com reviews, mostly from Christians, show the polarizing opinions. A quick tabulation of the responses show that 59 percent (405 out of 683) of the reviews are favorable, with four- to five-star ratings. There are 33 percent (224) unfavorable reviews, with one- to two-star ratings.[44] This polarization is unusual, because most product reviews, Bell's other books included, skew either toward the favorable side or the unfavorable side. In this case, although favorable reviews still outscore unfavorable ones, the U-shaped distribution shows that Bell has touched on a controversial topic among Christians with relatively strong support on both ends of the spectrum.

Therefore, I expect strong reactions from readers about this chapter. I ask those who have made up their minds regarding this matter to remember that, apart from the core beliefs of Christianity (such as those that are part of the commonly accepted Apostles' Creed), there have always been differing views regarding what the Bible teaches and how God relates to His creation. Those who disagree may all have biblically sound arguments while basing their interpretations on different frameworks.

In disagreeing, we must remember that it's impossible for our finite minds to fully comprehend our infinite God. We have to be cautious when claiming to fully understand God to the exclusion of others with a different viewpoint. I remember reading somewhere that every theologian is a heretic to a certain extent, because it's impossible for any one person to "corner the truth." With respect to the topics we will briefly discuss in this chapter, Christopher Marshall says it best:

> Maybe a humble agnosticism is the wisest option. How the destruction of all wickedness and the redemption of all things are to be effected is known only to God.[45]

I don't think it is good to be an agnostic, but when it comes to specific theological issues, especially with respect to issues that have generated enduring debates for centuries, it's better to maintain a healthy degree of humble agnosticism and admit that we just don't know for sure. Regardless of our personal convictions, we need to leave room for disagreement without accusing others of being heretics.

With that in mind, let's discuss this issue through two common "What about…?" questions. The first is based on the oft-quoted Hebrews 9:27–28:

> *And as it is appointed for men to die once, but after this the judgment, so Christ was offered once to bear the sins of many.* (NKJV)

The other is based on Matthew 25:41 and 46:

> *Then [the King] will also say to those on the left hand, "Depart from Me, you cursed, into the everlasting fire prepared for the devil and his angels…." And these will go away into everlasting punishment, but the righteous into eternal life.* (NKJV)

It will take two chapters to cover these two separate but related questions.

THE TRADITIONAL JUDGE-FIRST VIEW: JUDGMENT OR CONDEMNATION?

> *We use Hebrews 9:27 as a threat to tell people they need to reconcile with God through Christ in this life.*

When I share with others God's relentless parental love, one of the most common questions is, "What about God's judgment?" They then remind me of Hebrews 9:27. I've used this verse often, especially when sharing my faith with non-Christians, to show that I don't want to face God the judge after this life without receiving Christ as Savior, and neither should they. We use Hebrews 9:27 as a threat to tell people they need to reconcile with God through Christ in this life so they won't be condemned after this life.

It's important to note that this explanation assumes the word *judgment* in Hebrews 9:27 carries the same meaning as "condemnation" or "punishment." The assumption is that judgment brings punishment. When we share our faith like this, we're essentially telling our friends that unless they receive Jesus Christ as Savior, the automatic outcome of judgment is eternal death as a sentence from God. But Hebrews 9:27 says that we all face "judgment," *not* "condemnation." In judgment there is a decision to be made; it would be too presumptuous to say that it *must* result in eternal condemnation.

The word *judgment* used here is the Greek word *krisis*. A judgment can go either way—acquittal or condemnation. The traditional retributive justice framework leads many Christians to automatically interpret judgment as condemnation.

The automatic interpretation of *krisis* as condemnation (or punishment) is the result of stringing together Romans 3:23, Romans 6:23, and Hebrews 9:27. We assume that God administers *retributive* justice; based on this assumption, we construct a framework to convince others that everyone needs to receive Jesus Christ to avoid God's punishment.

LET'S DIG MORE DEEPLY: JUSTICE AND RIGHTEOUSNESS

Administering justice means making things right—that is, to bring about righteousness. In the Bible, justice and righteousness are closely related concepts.

As we attempt to understand biblical righteousness, we need to start from the concept of relational rightness through restorative justice to attain *shalom*. We cannot restrict our understanding only to the Greco-Roman concept of an abstract moral rightness or balance. We need to remember that *shalom* refers to a wholesome harmony among people in a community with God as the head of that community. Restorative justice is the attainment or restoration of *shalom*, and judgment is the way we decide how to get there.

> *Making the offender miserable doesn't restore the victim or shalom; it only adds to the total amount of misery in the world.*

Biblical judgment, therefore, is about restoration and reconciliation, not about retribution and punishment. When God judges, we cannot assume that His purpose is to balance the scale of retributive justice by making the offender suffer. God is interested in creating and restoring *shalom*, in making things whole again. God doesn't seek a destructive or punishing outcome. God seeks completeness, soundness, welfare, and peace in the context of a community of loving relationships. His justice is all about healing and restoring what has gone wrong with His creation, not about exacting proportional and eternal punishment from the offenders.

Indeed, God is holy, righteous, and just, but God's justice isn't the same as what the Greeks and the Romans thought of as justice. God's justice isn't about defending His own character by punishing the offender. God's justice is about fixing, repairing, and restoring what has gone wrong, creating and restoring *shalom*. Making the offender miserable doesn't restore the victim or *shalom*; it only adds to the total amount of misery in the world.

Instead of a God who adds misery to His creation by insisting on punishing all sinners, Jesus illustrates a different God in the famous parable of the Prodigal Son (Luke 15:11–24). Jesus tells this story to demonstrate our need for repentance, to turn away from sin and return to God's love. The prodigal son suffers from the wages of sin—from his own actions. The penalty comes from his own mistakes and from others who mistreat him, not from his father. In this story Jesus makes no mention of any retribution or penalty to uphold the father's dignity, justice, or righteousness, although the son has committed great wrong against his father. The son repents and returns to his father without worrying about having to face him as a judge. The prodigal son simply comes home to the father, who "saw him and was filled with compassion for him; he ran to his son, threw his arms around him and kissed him" (Luke 15:20, TNIV).

Throughout Luke 15 Jesus responded to the Pharisees and teachers of the law, who complained that Jesus welcomed sinners instead of judging and rejecting them. Jesus used the parables of the lost sheep, the lost coin, and the lost son to illustrate the concept of restorative justice. With respect to the lost son, the father adds joy and love to his lost son without first insisting on retribution and penalty for his sins. The father restores what has been lost through the son's rebellion and sins. This is biblical justice. Jesus uses this parable to show that the primary relationship between God and humankind is the parent-child relationship, not that of the punisher-offender.

God will, indeed, bring justice. God will right what is wrong and bring healing to the broken relationships among His people and His creation. This is God's justice.

THE PARENT-FIRST VIEW: THREAT OR PROMISE?

In view of what we've discussed so far, we need to revisit the meaning of Hebrews 9:27 within the framework of a parent-first God administering *restorative* justice. One thing we can do is review this verse in its context so that we understand how the word *judgment* is used in view of the theme being presented by the writer of Hebrews.

In Hebrews 9, the topic is the ministry of Jesus Christ as the eternal High Priest and Mediator of the new covenant. The passage is focused on Christ and the impacts of His sacrifice. The writer doesn't try to teach us how people are punished after their earthly lives. Rather, the

> *The writer of Hebrews shows us a promise that results from the sacrifice of Christ who bears our sins, not a threat if people don't receive Christ.*

writer shows us the difference between the ministry of the high priests of the first covenant and the ministry of Christ in the new covenant. The former is an annual sacrifice made by human high priests using the blood of animals to bring about imperfect redemption, and only for a period of time (Hebrews 9:6–10). The new covenant is a once-for-all sacrifice made by Christ with His own blood, bringing eternal redemption.

In this context the writer tells us that Christ brings permanent reconciliation between God and humanity (Hebrews 9:11–14). The writer speaks of "the promise of the eternal inheritance" (Hebrews 9:15) for those who have been called. The blood of Christ cleanses all sins for eternity, so that when we face God at the final judgment we're free from our sins (Hebrews 9:24–28). The writer of Hebrews shows us a *promise* that results from the sacrifice of Christ who bears our sins, not a *threat* if people don't receive Christ.

Therefore, we need to review *judgment* in the context of a promise, not a threat. Without any doubt the Bible teaches that everyone will face a day of judgment.[46] It's something we all have to experience. Traditionally, however, we've interpreted the final judgment as a threat. In pop culture, stories and movies about Judgment Day invariably portray violence, widespread calamity, death to millions, and a generally catastrophic ending.

This isn't what the Bible teaches about Judgment Day. Revelation tells of much trauma *leading up to* Judgment Day, but the end is a joyous event when all are restored. On Judgment Day, we face the judge who

made known to us the mystery of his will according to his good pleasure, which he purposed in Christ, to be put into effect when the times reach their fulfillment—to bring unity to all things in heaven and on earth under Christ. (Ephesians 1:9–10, TNIV)

Paul also writes in 1 Corinthians 4:3–5:

I do not even judge myself....He who judges me is the Lord. Therefore judge nothing before the time, until the Lord comes, who will both bring to light the hidden things of darkness and reveal the counsel of the hearts. Then each one's praise will come from God. (NKJV, emphasis added)

Paul doesn't take the time to talk about punishment for sinners. He tells his readers not to focus on judging the negatives in this life, but instead to focus on God's praise at the final judgment, when the Lord comes. Judgment Day will be a celebration of all God has done throughout history to bring about reconciliation between Him and His children. God will bring "unity to all things in heaven and on earth under Christ." It's the celebration of the ultimate *shalom*. God's focus is restoration, not retribution.

When we face judgment after this life, we face the restoration of all that is right. I don't think the writer of Hebrews intended to issue a threat or warning for non-Christians. Let's read the passage one more time, this time including the context:

And just as each person is destined to die once and after that comes judgment, so also Christ died once for all time as a sacrifice to take away the sins of many people. He will come again, not to deal with our sins, but to bring salvation to all who are eagerly waiting for him. (Hebrews 9:27–28, NLT)

The writer promises that because Christ bore our sins through His sacrifice, when we face judgment after our earthly life, those who are waiting for His return won't need to bear their sins anymore. What a wonderful promise!

THE FORK IN THE ROAD

So, here's another choice you can make with respect to Hebrews 9:27–28. Is it a threat or a promise? We can view it as a threat—that we don't want to face God's judgment without first becoming a Christian in this life—or we can view it as a promise from a relentlessly loving parent for those who are waiting for Christ to return. What's your preference?

After seeing Hebrews 9:27 as a promise to replace the traditional threat, my friends often ask about other references about God's eternal judgment. A commonly used passage is the division of sheep and goats in Matthew 25:31–46.

What About Hell?

ETERNAL JUDGMENT ACCORDING TO
MATTHEW 25:31–46

In this passage Jesus teaches the need for us to perform deeds of charity for the hungry, the thirsty, homeless strangers, the naked, the sick, and those in prison. Based on passages such as this, Mother Teresa built her legacy of compassion for millions around the world.

The NASB assigns the heading "The Judgment" to this passage. According to the content, I think a more appropriate heading would be "The Call for Compassion." The theme and focus of Jesus' teaching in Matthew 25 is that we should be compassionate to people who are in need.

Nonetheless, we need to address the topic of hell. There are five main issues: what hell is, who ends up there, how people end up there, how long hell lasts, and whether there's a way out. These questions have generated numerous debates over the centuries. It's an emotional topic for many, Christians and otherwise. Timothy Keller noted in his 2009 best seller, *The Reason for God*:

In our culture, divine judgment is one of Christianity's most offensive doctrines.[47]

I don't hope to resolve anything that has been controversial for as long as there have been Christians. I will, however, summarize the most popular views and state my preferences.

WHAT IS HELL?

There are two common views of hell. One describes a physical place of intense eternal suffering. The other describes not a physical place but a state of godless existence.

Those who view hell as a physical place base their view on the New Testament concept derived from the word *Gehenna*, the Hebrew name for a valley outside Jerusalem where sacrifices were made to pagan gods. This place came to be associated with hell because of the threats of judgment found in Jeremiah 7:32 and 19:6. Many view this as a place where God will dispose of His enemies and those who aren't His children.

Many metaphors lead to this conclusion, starting with Jesus' words in Matthew 25.

Depart from me, you who are accursed, into the eternal fire prepared for the devil and his angels.... Then they will go away to eternal punishment. (Matthew 25:41, 46)

We can find further fire-and-brimstone references to hell in Mark 9:43 and 48, Matthew 13:42 and 50, and in Revelation 20:15, where it's called "the lake of fire." Although this description has caused many writers and artists to describe punishment in hell, there isn't much biblical support for graphic depictions.

In addition to fire, hell is described as a place of utter darkness in Matthew 8:12, 22:13, and 25:30. Since fire and darkness don't physically go together, we can surmise that the Bible doesn't necessarily mean hell as a physical place of fire *and* darkness, but that these are metaphors of intense suffering and separation from God, who is the source of eternal bliss and light.

> *In eternity, when all worldly distractions and fleshly desires vanish, we're left with our most basic and fundamental object of desire: a relationship with God.*

This explanation leads us to the view that hell is a state of existence without God. Darkness is the absence of light. Darkness is not a "thing" as such but the lack of light. Light is a form of energy; the absence of this energy is darkness. So it is with hell along this line of reasoning. Although it is a state of intense suffering, some believe this suffering isn't really an imposition of any punishment but the absence of the object of one's deepest longing—God.

Christians agree that, whether we're aware of it or not, all humans need the love of God. Every one of us has a longing inside to relate to God in love. It may be suppressed and denied, but in eternity, when all worldly distractions and fleshly desires vanish, we're left with our most basic and fundamental desire: a relationship with God. Those who deny God will find this desire missing in the very core of their being. The thirst and pain that result from this unmet longing will burn like the hottest flame, and the deprivation of the presence of God will overwhelm like the deepest darkness. This is intense suffering, indeed. I don't think God needs to add any fire and brimstone to intensify such impossibly extreme longing and thirst.

Before we were married, my wife and I had to endure several months of a long-distance relationship when I was in Canada and she was in the United States. This was more decades ago than I would like to count. Back then long-distance landline calls were our only form of "live" interaction. Flying was relatively expensive. There was no e-mail or mobile phones. Although we tried to stay in contact often, there was no way for us to know what the other was doing all the time. Some evenings when I didn't know where she was and there was no answer on her line (there was no voicemail back then, either), I would go crazy and call every few minutes, letting it ring and ring. Finally, when she answered I'd let out a sigh of relief. The longing to connect with her, even if only through the telephone, was met. Until that moment I was restless and anxious.

This is a very limited example of our deep longing for God. We can imagine this longing multiplied by a million times, but that would still be inadequate to describe the longing for God's loving presence. In hell this longing will *never* be met. When those who reject God realize how desolate existence is without His loving presence, the unmet longing will burn hotter than the hottest flame. The loneliness will be darker than the deepest abyss. The realization that their unmet longing will last forever will be unimaginably tragic, beyond any description and understanding.

Whether or not hell is a physical place, there is a belief that in hell all persons maintain their identity and will have a conscious awareness of their existence into eternity. There is also a view called annihilationism, which teaches that hell is where a soul loses its self-awareness and becomes nothing after earthly death.[48] This isn't very common among Christians because of their belief in an eternal identity for every human. Generally speaking, Christians don't adopt a view that promotes the concept of "eternal nothingness." In all cases, however, God's presence is not in hell.

WHO GOES TO HELL?

This question, a hotly contested topic that has generated debate for centuries, is what started me on this journey of writing this book. Most of us appreciate certainty. Some may enjoy ambiguity and questions, but most of us prefer clarity and answers. It applies to many areas in life, including our financial security, relationships, and eternal destiny. That's why we like to have a nice bank account and steady income, committed and loving relationships, and a surefire ticket to heaven.

Many religious leaders try to tell us how we can get into heaven to enjoy eternal bliss and avoid everlasting torture in hell. With the exception of Buddhism, which advocates a return after this earthly life to eternal nothingness as a drop of water returns to the ocean, most major religions attempt to show how we can find our way to heaven and avoid the road to hell. Many feel Christianity is no different from other religions in this aspect.

Most view hell as the opposite of heaven. There's no in-between after this life ends. A person who dies goes to either heaven or hell. In terms of who goes where—and to summarize the Christian view at the risk of oversimplifying—there are three camps of thought: universalism, exclusivism, and inclusivism.

Universalism teaches that all are saved through the sacrifice of Christ, although most don't know it yet.[49] Proponents of this school of thought teach that no one is unredeemable. In His mercy, God will eventually redeem every soul and reconcile through Christ all humankind into God's presence.

There are strengths and weaknesses to universalism. One strength is that it shows an all-loving and forgiving God who reconciles with humankind at great cost to Himself. The most obvious weakness to many is the repugnance that historical monsters such as brutal dictators, indiscriminate terrorists, and unrepentant mass murderers might share eternal forgiveness with their countless victims.

The other extreme school of thought is exclusivism, which teaches that unless one makes a deliberate and conscious decision to receive Christ's gift of salvation in this life (to be "born again"), one goes to hell. If one does not make that choice, there's no recourse after the end of this life. The person will suffer in hell eternally. The form of receiving the gift of salvation may vary, but exclusivism essentially guarantees a sincerely repentant sinner entrance into heaven after making a decision, usually through some kind of "sinner's prayer." This view is adopted by most evangelicals.

The following joke may shed some light on how other people view the exclusivism doctrine:

A man arrives at the gates of heaven. St. Peter asks, "Religion?"
The man says, "Roman Catholic."
St. Peter looks down his list, and says, "Go to room 24, but be very quiet as you pass room 8."
Another man arrives at the gates of heaven. "Religion?"
"Buddhism."
"Go to room 18, but be very quiet as you pass room 8."
A third man arrives at the gates. "Religion?"
"Jewish."
"Go to room 11, but be very quiet as you pass room 8."

The man says, "I can understand there being different rooms for different religions, but why must I be quiet when I pass room 8?"

St. Peter tells him, "Well the exclusive evangelicals are in room 8, and they think they're the only ones here."[50]

There are strengths and weaknesses for exclusivism. One strength is the certainty of eternal salvation after making a clear choice. Another is that it drives evangelistic zeal in its adherents to save as many as possible by telling others how to receive Christ. One weakness is that the proponents have to explain what to do with those who are too young or lacking the mental facility to make a choice.

The "age of accountability" theory says that a person needs to reach a certain level of intellectual, emotional, and spiritual maturity in order to understand the meaning of receiving Christ. Most people suppose this maturity happens during the teen years. However, many of us know children who have received Jesus into their lives in childhood. Do these decisions count? Will they need to recommit when they're older? When a young person dies before making a decision for or against Christ, how do we know whether he or she has reached the age of accountability?

> *Inclusivism portrays a God who is fair and ultimately compassionate, who honors each person's choice.*

There is also a question about one's level of IQ. Regardless of age some simply don't have the mental facility to make an independent decision of this nature. The cause may be birth defects, genetics, illness, or other unfortunate circumstances. I read somewhere that in the United States it isn't possible to convict someone with an IQ below 80 of first-degree murder because of the presumed lack of ability to make a clear moral choice between what's right and wrong. What IQ does God require before he decides whether a person is intelligent enough to make a decision for or against Christ?

These two concepts introduce uncertainty regarding who goes to heaven and who goes to hell. Similarly, it's difficult to come up with a satisfactory response to those who ask about people who never have a chance to hear about Jesus Christ in their earthly lives, such as those in regions where Christianity is unheard of. Unless exclusivism adherents are willing to accept the concept that these people all end up in hell, they have to embrace principles of inclusivism, at least to some extent.

Inclusivism occupies the huge middle ground between the two extremes. Simply stated, it essentially says, "I don't know, but God knows, and that's good enough for me." Inclusivists tend not to insist that it's necessary for every human to make a conscious decision *in this life* to receive Christ in order to avoid hell and enter into the presence of God in eternity. There are many opportunities for a person to experience God and submit to God, whether one is directly and consciously exposed to Christianity or not.

Inclusivism portrays a God who is fair and ultimately compassionate, who honors each person's choice. Some proponents of inclusivism may believe that this life is the only opportunity to make a decision for God, and others may accept opportunities after this life and before the final judgment. Most accept that there's no one in heaven who doesn't want to be there and there's no one in hell who doesn't choose to be there.

Inclusivism relieves us of the need to assess who goes to heaven and who goes to hell. Instead, Christians should focus on submitting to God's will and calling. There are many things Christians can do—such as deeds of compassion for the poor and marginalized, caring for one another, visiting those in prison, witnessing for Christ, and making disciples for Christ. The list of such callings is almost endless. Christians can keep themselves occupied in carrying out God's callings and leave to God the issue of other people's eternal destiny.

One of the difficulties with inclusivism is the uncertainty of an individual's eternal destiny. People want clarity. "Only God knows" is a concept many find difficult to accept. Evangelicals especially like the certainty of a transaction; if someone says a prayer of repentance and submits to Jesus sincerely, it's a done deal. Leaving it up to God during or after this life is too uncertain. Besides, the thought of non-Christians, even after they've been exposed to and rejected faith in this life, going to heaven makes some people wonder why they would even bother to evangelize and tell others about the good news of Jesus Christ.

Exclusivists often accuse universalists and inclusivists of degrading or cheapening the saving grace of Jesus Christ. If it's unnecessary for a person to consciously receive in this life the gift of salvation to avoid going to hell, then Christ died for nothing.

I find this line of reasoning faulty. If anything, universalists and inclusivists *increase* the worth of the work of Christ by including more who would benefit from it. If the ministry of Christ rescues, say, seventy percent—or even a hundred percent—of humanity, it is more worthy and precious than if it rescues only, say, ten percent of humanity. It seems unreasonable for exclusivists to accuse inclusivists or universalists of cheapening the work of Jesus Christ. The ministry of Christ is more precious and worthy when more are saved.

Those are the three schools of thought. I think inclusivism makes the most sense.

HOW DOES ONE END UP IN HELL?

> *All that are in Hell, choose it. Without that self-choice, there can be no Hell."* —C.S. Lewis

Many Christians believe that a person ends up in hell because of God's judgment against those who aren't Christians, or at least those who oppose God. As a result God casts them into hell. This view is well known and teaches that all who are disqualified for heaven end up in hell because God puts them there. They're cast into hell as their well-deserved consequence for the choices they've either made or failed to make during their earthly lives. At the end of their lives God makes a judgment, and they go one way or the other for eternity, whether they like it or not.

Others believe hell exists because of God's respect for free will for every human. C.S. Lewis expresses his view about those who choose joyful submission to God and those who have their own way in hell:

> There are only two kinds of people in the end: those who say to God, "Thy will be done," and those to whom God says, in the

end, "*Thy* will be done." All that are in Hell, choose it. Without that self-choice, there can be no Hell. No soul that seriously and constantly desires joy will ever miss it. Those who seek find. To those who knock, it is open.[51]

Timothy Keller, author of *The Reason for God*, agrees:

Hell…is the trajectory of a soul, living a self-absorbed, self-centered life, going on and on forever….In short, hell is simply one's freely chosen identity apart from God on a trajectory into infinity….It is a travesty to picture God casting people into a pit who are crying "I'm sorry! Let me out!"[52]

It's safe to say most Christians believe God will judge at the end of time and make all things right. That includes every soul's eternal destiny. There are different opinions about whether decisions are based solely on a person's deeds and decisions in this life, or whether there's a second chance after this life and before the end of time.

These are difficult issues to resolve. Theologians over the centuries haven't resolved them to unanimity. The chief argument against the exclusivism theory is that eternity is infinite; it would be difficult to accept that our eternal destiny is based only on what we do or choose during our short span of earthly life. On the other hand, there are strong arguments against the inclusivism theory. For instance, if there's a second chance after this life, then why not a third or fourth and into infinity, since eternity is timeless? If that's the case, what's the use of making any decisions for God or people, now or whenever?

I feel the exclusivism theory is too harsh. One of the disciples, the famous Doubting Thomas, didn't believe in the resurrection of Christ. Instead of judging him, Jesus Christ appeared to him personally and let Thomas touch His wounds. Thomas believed and worshipped as a result (John 20:24–28). But what if Thomas got run over by an oxcart before Christ appeared to him and didn't have a chance to change his mind? Would he have ended up in hell for his refusal to believe in Christ's resurrection?

Thomas had been a disciple of Christ for years. He had observed many miracles. The other disciples, his close friends, were ecstatic about the resurrection of their Master. Thomas still refused to believe. If Christ were kind enough to personally convince him, it's difficult to reason why Christ wouldn't offer at least one afterlife opportunity to billions others who have had fewer opportunities, if any, to know Him during their earthly lives.

For ten years I frequently, often weekly, flew in and out of Toronto for my work. I rode regularly with one taxi driver, George, for my trips between home and the airport. He was Greek Orthodox and had a deep faith.

George once told me a story about his father-in-law, who wasn't only an atheist but a communist as well. George spent many evenings over coffee or ouzo arguing faith and politics with him. They would go on for hours, often past midnight, discussing whether God existed and never came to agreement. The father-in-law fell ill and eventually went into a coma. George and his wife visited him often.

One day, about five weeks into his coma, George and his wife arrived for their regular visit. When they entered the room, his father-in-law suddenly woke up, sat up in bed, and said, "You gotta believe in God! You gotta believe in Christ!" Afterward, according to George, his father-in-law appeared to be at peace. He soon fell back into a coma and passed away.

In his coma George's father-in-law must have been given another opportunity to believe in God. I don't know what happens in a coma physiologically and spiritually, but from a human perspective a person in a coma is unconscious and shouldn't be able to consciously make a decision whether to trust God or not. But something happened during the father-in-law's coma for him to change his mind about God. Did God somehow reach his mind and reveal Christ to him?

HOW LONG DOES HELL LAST?

When Jesus speaks of the destination of goats (those who don't carry out the deeds of compassion), he says:

"Depart from me, you who are cursed, into the eternal fire prepared for the devil and his angels...." Then they will go away to eternal punishment, but the righteous to eternal life. (Matthew 25:41,46, TNIV)

Jesus uses the word *eternal* twice in this passage. Although it's possible to interpret *eternal* as referring to a long period of time and not necessarily a never-ending one, it's more appropriate to understand it as an unending duration. With respect to the eternal fire and punishment Jesus speaks of, I agree with the traditional understanding that Jesus speaks of a place or state of existence of unending suffering. This is what hell means.

There are some related questions. When does hell start? Is there an end to hell in God's plan? If hell never ends, can anyone who's in hell escape from it?

WHEN DOES HELL START?

Some believe hell starts after this earthly life. Indeed, many passages in the Bible talk about going to or being cast into a place or state of intense suffering characterized by darkness, fire, gnashing of teeth, thirst, and so on. Although agreeing to the afterlife hell, some believe hell starts with our earthly life. As long as we live a life without the presence of God, we are in hell, here and thereafter.

I want to tell the story of two sisters who are both in their eighties. Both are in poor health. One, Tina, has terminal cancer and has been near death more than once. At the time of this writing, her cancer is stabilized and she enjoys having her children and grandchildren around. She's surrounded by loving relationships. Her two sons and a daughter as well as their families live nearby and attend to her needs lovingly. Even out-of-town grandchildren visit often.

Her sister, Rita, lives alone in another part of town, five minutes away by car. Rita isn't healthy, but she has no known life-threatening diseases and is able to drive. However, she hardly talks to anyone throughout the day. Her conversations, whether on the phone or in person, are mostly negative. Rita's always complaining about someone or something. Although she was born in the same town and has lived there for more than eighty years, she has no friends or relatives who regularly speak with or visit her; she has chased everyone away through her complaints and bitterness. She complains that no one calls her, but she refuses to call anyone, except to complain. The only driving she does is to the doctor or to the stores, never to visit friends or relatives.

Rita and Tina aren't on speaking terms because of a quarrel that started more than fifty years ago about some family property. Rita thinks Tina took advantage of her and has never forgiven her. When Tina was near death several months ago with cancer, Rita cursed her and told her that God was judging her, that she would go to hell because of the disputed property. Rita rained curses not only on Tina personally, but also through Tina's family members. Rita complains about her postman, her neighbors, the people who come to fix her appliances, the cable TV service people, call center employees, and pretty much everyone she comes in contact with, including her two daughters. No one dares call her for fear of being yelled at. Only one daughter loves her enough to endure the torrent of negativism and speak with her daily. The other daughter rarely calls. Her out-of-town grandchildren seldom visit, even though they often vacation at a timeshare just an hour away.

Despite repeated pleas from the one daughter to forgive and forget, Rita steadfastly holds on to her bitterness and hatred. Rita has numerous ailments, real and imagined, and is in severe pain daily. My wife and I speculate that much of her pain and ailments are the result of bitterness and anger.

In contrast, Tina, with her diabetes and cancer, told my wife that she was surrounded by such love that she felt as though she were in heaven. She has always been a cheerful and reliable person, and people enjoy being in her company. She treasures each day and continues to express love to those around her. She doesn't know how long she has to live, but as far as she's concerned, she's already in heaven. She would love to reconcile with Rita, but the pain of Rita's curses still stings, and she knows Rita hasn't forgiven her.

I don't know what eternal destiny awaits Tina and Rita. Tina has faced imminent death and counts her earthly days as blessings. She feels she's in heaven, giving and receiving loving relationships. In stark contrast, Rita is living in a hell of her own creation, shooting fiery darts of bitterness and pain and isolated from loving relationships. Although her daughter continues to beg Rita to reconcile with her dying sister, who is only a phone call or five-minute drive away, she refuses to do so. She even accuses her daughter of betraying her, because her daughter refuses to join in her hatred for Tina and her family. Physically, she has no life. As far as I understand, she's already in hell. We hope and pray that Rita finds release from hell through faith in Christ and forgiveness.

Whenever hell starts, we need to address whether it ends. There are two major camps. One advocates that notwithstanding the use of the word *eternity*, other Bible passages show that because of the love of God, which is more enduring than sin and suffering, God will eventually rescue all who are in hell to complete God's plan of redemption for all creation. The biblical basis of this view is similar to that of universalism. The other camp believes that hell, like heaven, is unending.

CAN SOMEONE IN HELL EVENTUALLY GET OUT?

Obviously, for those who advocate a final redemption that destroys hell, this isn't an issue, for God will bring an end to hell, redeeming all who are in it. This is essentially another form of universalism. For those who believe in an everlasting hell, we need to discuss whether it's possible to get out of hell after a soul is in it.

The basic principles between the disagreeing parties are similar to those who disagree over whether hell is eternal. Those who advocate an exit base their understanding on the unending love of God. Those who advocate no exit base it on the need for eternal punishment for offending the eternal God. The key arguments are similar to those about how one ends up in hell, whether God gives only one chance in this life or more opportunities after our earthly lives. If I choose to reject God in this life, can I change my mind after this life? If I choose to reject Him a second time, do I get a third, fourth, or infinite opportunities into eternity? This issue is definitely problematic.

In my opinion, it is unnecessary for the proponents of the afterlife judgment to extend beyond the second chance. The Bible teaches in passages such as Hebrews 9:27 and Revelation 19:17–21 that there is a final judgment after this life. As we discussed earlier, this is a time of *judgment*, not necessarily *condemnation*. After that, we enter into eternity based on the final judgment.

I believe there's a second and final chance for a person to trust God after this life. Every person should get an opportunity similar to what Christ offered Thomas, leaving no doubt about the extent to which God goes to reconcile each child back to His love through Christ. At that one final time, when all doubts are gone and everyone is on the same footing and clarity of understanding—unaffected by cultural background, circumstances, and life experiences—the choice will be final.

THE FORK IN THE ROAD

> *It wouldn't be productive for an adherent of any view, or combination of views, to claim exclusivity and declare disagreeable ones as heresies.*

Hell is associated with the final destiny of every human. After all is said and done, fantasies and fairytales notwithstanding, earthly death is inevitable. Since Christians believe in a never-ending afterlife, how we live this afterlife is more important than how we spend our earthly lives. Many endure hardship in this life for the hope of a better afterlife. It's horrible to entertain the thought that anyone, ourselves included, could be in torment for eternity after this life, which is tough enough. Nonetheless, I think we've touched on most of the common views.

Though I've stated my own preferences, each view has its own biblical basis. It wouldn't be productive for an adherent of any view, or combination of views, to claim exclusivity and declare disagreeable ones as heresies. Many will differ from my preferences. My choices are based on the framework of a parent-first God who creates each human with an eternal soul whom He loves relentlessly. Love must be voluntary, and that applies to all humans in eternity. God respects the choices we make because He didn't create mindless robots or coerced slaves.

At the end, however, God is God and He'll make His judgment based on *shalom*—restorative justice. Those who accept the love of God will enjoy peace with God. Others are determined to reject God's love, and He will allow them to spend their eternity in a godless and loveless existence: hell. These convictions guide me to my choices. What are your convictions, and what are your choices?

What About the Suffering Messiah in Isaiah 53?

ELEVEN

Many people point to Isaiah 53:6 as the key verse explaining how the suffering Messiah takes on the punishments for our sins. Because of the traditional view of God as an immovable judge administering inflexible retributive justice, most readers interpret Isaiah 53 as proof that God imposes His punishments on the Messiah because of our sins. However, a more careful reading shows that this isn't necessarily true.

Let's look at Isaiah 53:4–10, which describes the Messiah's suffering:

> *Surely He has borne our griefs*
> *And carried our sorrows;*
> *Yet we esteemed Him stricken,*
> *Smitten by God, and afflicted.*
> *But He was wounded for our transgressions,*
> *He was bruised for our iniquities;*
> *The chastisement for our peace was upon Him,*
> *And by His stripes we are healed.*

All we like sheep have gone astray;
We have turned, every one, to his own way;
And the Lord has laid on Him the iniquity of us all.
He was oppressed and He was afflicted,
Yet He opened not His mouth;
He was led as a lamb to the slaughter,
And as a sheep before its shearers is silent,
So He opened not His mouth.
He was taken from prison and from judgment,
And who will declare His generation?
For He was cut off from the land of the living;
For the transgressions of My people He was stricken.
And they made His grave with the wicked—
But with the rich at His death,
Because He had done no violence,
Nor was any deceit in His mouth.
Yet it pleased the Lord to bruise Him;
He has put Him to grief.
When You make His soul an offering for sin,
He shall see His seed, He shall prolong His days,
And the pleasure of the Lord shall prosper in His hand. (NKJV)

Without question someone significant suffered for our sins. Traditionally, many Christians take it as a foregone conclusion that this passage describes the Messiah suffering punishments imposed by God. However, if we read this passage carefully without the preconception of God as an immovable judge administering inflexible retributive justice, we may see that our sin is the source of the suffering, consistent with the other forks in the road we have discovered so far in this book.

LET'S DIG MORE DEEPLY: WHO CRUCIFIED JESUS?

Most are familiar with the biblical account of the crucifixion of Jesus Christ. I want to focus on one issue: who put Jesus to death? The answer is obvious: people did. The Bible tells us who took accountability for the crucifixion. Peter spoke to the crowd in Jerusalem in Acts 2. It was the first recorded sermon from a church leader in the Bible. In the following verses, we can read Peter's conclusion and the people's response to it:

> *[Peter addressed the crowd:] "Therefore let all the house of Israel know assuredly that God has made this Jesus,* whom you crucified, *both Lord and Christ."*
>
> Now when they heard this, they were cut to the heart, *and said to Peter and the rest of the apostles, "Men and brethren, what shall we do?"*
>
> *Then Peter said to them, "Repent, and let every one of you be baptized in the name of Jesus Christ for the remission of sins; and you shall receive the gift of the Holy Spirit. For the promise is to you and to your children, and to all who are afar off, as many as the Lord our God will call."*
>
> *And with many other words he testified and exhorted them, saying, "Be saved from this perverse generation." Then those who gladly received his word were baptized; and that day about three thousand souls were added to them.* (Acts 2:36–41, NKJV, emphasis added)

Peter put the accountability for crucifying Jesus squarely on people—*this Jesus, whom you crucified*—and they accepted the accountability—*they were cut to the heart*. People, not God, imposed the death penalty on Jesus Christ, the Messiah.

Therefore, we are the ones who impose the wages of sin on Christ. Keep in mind that God decided before the creation of the world to bear our sins through Jesus Christ (Ephesians 1:4-8), so He could restore *shalom* and bring reconciliation, healing, and peace to His children and all creation at infinite cost to Himself. With this in mind, we can examine Isaiah 53:4–6.

> *Surely He has borne our griefs and carried our sorrows; yet we esteemed Him stricken, smitten by God, and afflicted.* (Isaiah 53:4, NKJV)

The first part of the verse does *not* speak of God's punishment. It speaks of our griefs and sorrows. The second half is interesting. It is *we*—humans—who esteemed (NASB, NKJV) or considered (NIV) Him stricken and smitten by God. The Bible doesn't say God did it. It says *we* considered the Messiah stricken, smitten, and afflicted by God. We don't need to blame God for the source of the suffering. Isaiah wrote that *we considered* the Messiah to be punished by God.

> *But He was wounded for* our *transgressions, He was bruised for* our *iniquities; the chastisement* for our peace *was upon Him, and by His stripes we are healed.* (Isaiah 53:5, emphasis added)

This shows that the sources of the Messiah's suffering were *our* transgressions and *our* iniquities. The chastisement was *for our peace*, and that by His stripes *we are healed*. The focus is *shalom*, healing, and relational peace for us and the community, and with God. It's about reconciliation and healing, not the appeasement of an angry God bent on punishing those who sin against Him. We do offend God when we sin, of course, but God doesn't operate by punishing us to appease Himself. God wants to restore peace and bring healing as a relentlessly loving parent.

> *All we like sheep have gone astray; we have turned, every one, to his own way; and the Lord has laid on Him the iniquity of us all.* (Isaiah 53:6)

THE PARENT-FIRST VIEW

God has lain on the Messiah the iniquity of us all. Again, in the framework of an immovable judge administering inflexible retributive justice, we can view this as God punishing the Messiah. However, in the framework of a relentlessly loving parent administering restorative justice, we can view this as God *redirecting* toward the Messiah the misery *we* cause. It's important to make the distinction between two very different actions. One is God *demanding* punishment that God imposes; the other is God *redirecting* consequences that sinners cause.

When I read this passage, I picture myself crossing a road. As an oncoming truck bears down on me, someone sees my imminent danger, pushes me out of the way, and gets crushed on my behalf. He gives his life to save mine.

Similarly, this is what the Messiah does for me. God comes in human flesh and takes the consequences of my sin. Whether it's the consequence of my carelessness in crossing the road without paying attention to the traffic, or a drunken truck driver ignoring his training and legal requirements, or both, I face death and someone takes my place by redirecting the consequence upon himself.

God comes in the flesh as Jesus Christ to bear the penalty of sin on our behalf, but the penalty comes not from God; it comes from humans. My rescuer's death is brought on by my own carelessness and that of the driver. Similarly, our iniquity brings pain and suffering. Although God redirected the pain and suffering to the Messiah, the source is the iniquity of us all, not a judiciary sentence from God. God redirects the consequences of our iniquity upon Himself through the suffering Messiah. That's how I understand Isaiah 53:6.

> *Although God redirected the pain and suffering to the Messiah, the source is the iniquity of us all, not a judiciary sentence from God.*

We can interpret the rest of Isaiah 53 along the same vein, according to the framework of a relentlessly loving parent administering restorative justice. The focus, therefore, isn't on the suffering Messiah bearing God's punishment for us; the focus is on how our sin causes the sufferings God takes on through the Messiah. One view leads us to see a judge punishing the suffering Messiah, who is God Himself in human form, and the other view leads us to see the Messiah bringing us life through His suffering:

After he has suffered, he will see the light of life and be satisfied; by his knowledge my righteous servant will justify many, and he will bear their iniquities. Therefore I will give him a portion among the great, and he will divide the spoils with the strong, because he poured out his life unto death, and was numbered with the transgressors. For he bore the sin of many, and made intercession for the transgressors. (Isaiah 53:11–12, TNIV)

THE FORK IN THE ROAD

In trying to understand Isaiah 53, we arrive at another fork in the road. Instead of the traditional view of the suffering Messiah who took on the penalty imposed by God, we can take the view that the Messiah suffered because he took on the penalty humans impose on ourselves, each other, and ultimately on God. Through this act of infinite love and humility, God through Christ forever absorbed the wages of sin, resulting in our freedom to forgive and be forgiven.

When I taught this lesson at a Sunday service at our church (I use an interactive teaching style), one of the mothers commented, "If my children disobeyed me, did something wrong and died, I would do anything within my power to bring them back to life."

This is *exactly* what God has done. He stopped at nothing, including giving Himself to the ugliness and horror of our sin through death, absorbing all the penalties, so we could receive and offer forgiveness. God then demonstrated His victory over sin and death by rising again through the power of the Holy Spirit, offering us the same resurrection power so we could receive life from Him and live again.

We can choose to see Isaiah 53 as the depiction of the suffering Messiah taking on God's punishment on our behalf because there's an immovable judge administering inflexible retributive justice, or we can choose the explanation of the suffering Messiah taking on the pain, suffering, and death we cause because there's a relentlessly loving parent administering restorative justice. I choose the parent.

What's your choice?

There's one more "What about…?" question we need to respond to before we complete our quest: Doesn't the Bible tell us there can be no forgiveness of sin without the shedding of blood, and doesn't that mean God insists on punishment before He can forgive?

What About Blood and Forgiveness in Hebrews 9:22?

TWELVE

THE TRADITIONAL JUDGE-FIRST VIEW

What about where the Bible says that without the shedding of blood there is no forgiveness (or remission) of sin? This is one of the most common "What about…?" questions. People usually ask about this verse from the understanding that blood-shedding represents suffering, and this verse teaches the need for God to punish before He can forgive. The implication is that Christ shed His blood on the cross on behalf of all sinners, satisfying the requirement for punishment and achieving forgiveness for those who put their faith in Jesus Christ's substitutionary sacrifice.

Interestingly, people usually quote just the second half of the verse. The complete verse goes like this:

> *And according to the law almost all things are purified with blood, and without shedding of blood there is no remission.* (Hebrews 9:22, NKJV)[53]

Further, in the wider context of Hebrews 9, the focus is on the cleansing power of blood, not on punishment, suffering, or death.

Granted, the sacrificial lamb (or goat or calf) needs to die in order to give its blood, and dying is indeed painful. In this context, however, the subject of the Bible passage is the cleansing power of blood, not the pain and suffering.

Numerous volumes have been written about this subject. I'll limit our discussion to an overview of the biblical view of blood and how it applies to this verse. My main objective is to show that Hebrews 9:22 doesn't tell us God must punish through the shedding of blood before He can forgive.

LET'S DIG MORE DEEPLY: THE PURPOSE OF BLOOD

Blood is a central symbol of the Christian faith. I'd like to take us through an overview of what the Bible teaches regarding the meaning of blood within the context of our relationship with God.

The book *In His Image*, coauthored by Paul Brand and Phillip Yancey, contains a section on blood comprising five chapters. Similarly, *The Incredible Machine*, a beautifully illustrated coffee table book from the National Geographic Society, devotes fifty-seven pages to a chapter entitled "The Powerful River," which describes the role blood plays in the human body.

Life is in blood. Without blood, there is no life. We read in Leviticus 17:14, "For the life of every creature is its blood: its blood is its life" (ESV). The association between blood and life is comparable to the relationship between water and life:

> Earthly rivers refresh the land with water; the body's stream nourishes and cleanses, delivering food and oxygen to every cell, removing wastes, regulating the human environment.[54]

However, we have learned to associate blood with suffering and violence, primarily because when we see the shedding of blood, it's usually from a wound or other painful events.

On the one hand, many of us find blood revolting. At least, it makes us uneasy. On the other hand, blood is critical to life, physiologically and spiritually. There are hundreds of mentions of blood in the Bible. Except for accounts of battles, blood in the Bible symbolizes life, not violence or suffering. When Jesus mentions blood, he refers mostly to the blood of the prophets and His own in the context of being the blood of the new covenant (see Matthew 23, Matthew 26, Mark 14, Luke 11, Luke 22, and John 6).

Blood performs many functions in our body. In this chapter we'll focus on just two major functions: cleansing and nourishing. We'll describe the physical functions and then draw biblical parallels to the spiritual functions of blood in the Christian life.

THE CLEANSING POWER OF BLOOD

Paul Brand suggests a simple experiment. With the help of a friend, he asks the reader to stop the flow of blood in the arm by tying a cuff around the upper arm, then performing an easy task such as flexing the fingers or making a fist many times in succession. He describes what would happen:

> The first few movements seem quite normal at first as the muscles obediently contract and relax. Then you feel a slight weakness. Almost without warning, after perhaps ten movements, a hot flash of pain strikes. Your muscles cramp violently. If you force yourself to continue the simple task, you will likely cry out in absolute agony. Finally, you cannot force yourself to continue; the pain overwhelms you.
>
> When you release the tourniquet…blood rushes into your aching arm and a wonderful soothing sense of relief floods your muscles….Physiologically, you have just experienced the cleansing power of blood.
>
> The pain came because you forced your muscles to keep working while the blood supply to your arm was shut off. As muscles converted oxygen into energy, they produced certain waste products [metabolites] that normally would have been flushed away instantly in the blood stream. Because of the constricted bloodflow, however, these metabolites accumulated in your cells. They were not *cleansed* by the swirling stream of blood,

and therefore in a few minutes you felt the agony of retained toxins.[55]

The Bible teaches about how the power of blood cleanses us from our spiritual poison—sin. In Hebrews 9 we read that the high priest can enter the inner room of the temple only after he offers blood. However, Christ

entered the Most Holy Place once and for all by his own blood, thus obtaining eternal redemption. The blood of goats and bulls... sprinkled on those who are ceremonially unclean sanctify them so that they are outwardly clean. How much more, then, will the blood of Christ...cleanse our consciences from acts that lead to death, so that we may serve the living God! (Hebrews 9:12–14, TNIV)

Many other passages illustrate the cleansing power of blood, from Leviticus to Revelation. In Leviticus 14, for example, a priest sprinkles cleansing blood on a person with an infectious skin disease and on the mildewed walls of a house.

These are they who have...washed their robes and made them white in the blood of the Lamb. (Revelation 7:14, TNIV)

> *Communion demonstrates my constant need for His Spirit to work in my life, cleansing me of my sins and empowering me.*

When a person becomes a Christian, he or she starts a new life. This is more like a U-turn toward God and an abandonment of selfish pursuits than an instant attainment of godly perfection. It's a lifelong process that starts with a spiritual rebirth followed by growth and maturation. We cannot instantly expect a totally sinless life after we receive Christ. We become more godly as we grow spiritually, but we don't become sinless overnight. In other words, the poisonous results of sin continue to accumulate in our lives, causing pain and sorrow to ourselves and those around us. That's why we need to have faith in Jesus—not only for our one-time rebirth but also for our daily lives.

This realization allows me to attach new meaning to communion. When I take communion, I take in the cleansing power of Christ. Communion doesn't symbolize only the suffering of Christ, although He suffered on my behalf the ugly outcomes of my sins. Communion also demonstrates my constant need for His Spirit to work in my life, cleansing me of my sins and empowering me, similar to the way my blood cleanses and nourishes my body. The Bible teaches that

> *the blood of Jesus…purifies us from all sin.…If we confess our sins, he is faithful and just and will forgive us our sins and purify us from all unrighteousness.* (1 John 1:7, 9, TNIV)

While physical blood cleanses our physical bodies, the blood of Jesus cleanses us spiritually.

This subject reminds me of the unrelenting love of God as my Father in heaven, a love He expresses through Christ. God knows I'm imperfect, and He provides for my imperfection through the cleansing blood of Christ. When I read "without the shedding of blood there is no remission" (NKJV), I feel encouraged to release my burden and weariness—the poisons of my life—by confessing that I've sinned against others and God, thus receiving by faith the cleansing blood of Christ. This fills me with thankfulness and hope to start living for Him anew.

Remembering the shed blood of Jesus gives me faith that He has the power to cleanse me of my unrighteousness, encouraging me to clean up my act by yielding to and following Him.

Instead of telling us that God requires the shedding of blood by punishing Christ before He can forgive, Hebrews 9:22 tells us that the blood of Christ cleanses us from our sins so we can give and receive forgiveness and be relieved of the burdens of sin.

THE LIFE-NOURISHING POWER OF BLOOD

Every 60 seconds, 1,440 times a day, our blood cycles through the body…traveling the double loop…known as the cardiovascular system.[56]

In addition to carrying away poison from our cells, blood brings nutrients to nourish the trillions of cells in our bodies. The most notable "cargo" carried in our bloodstream is oxygen, which is fuel for the body. Further, blood carries a perfect balance of minerals and salts; every element in its proper proportion is essential for the body.

So critical is this balance that a decline in the population of any one element can endanger life.[57]

I can think of no better way to describe how blood nourishes the body than the way Brand and Yancey describe this life-giving process:

Imagine an enormous tube snaking southward from Canada through the Amazon delta, plunging into oceans only to surface at every inhabited island, shooting out eastward through every jungle, plain, and desert in Africa, forking near Egypt to join all of Europe and Russia as well as the entire Middle East and Asia—a pipeline so global and pervasive that it links every person worldwide. Inside that tube an endless plenitude of treasures floats along on rafts: mangoes, coconuts, asparagus, and produce from every continent; watches, calculators, and cameras; gems and minerals; forty-nine brands of cereals; all styles and sizes of clothing; the contents of entire shopping centers. [Billions of] people have access: at a moment of need or want, they simply reach into the tube and seize whatever product suits them. Somewhere far down the pipeline a replacement is manufactured and inserted.

Such a pipeline exists inside each one of us, servicing not [six billion] but one hundred trillion cells in the human body. An endless supply of oxygen, amino acids, nitrogen, sodium potassium, calcium, magnesium, sugars, lipids, cholesterols, and hormones surges past our cells, carried on blood cell rafts or suspended in the fluid. Each cell has special withdrawal privileges to gather the resources needed to fuel a tiny engine for its complex chemical reactions.

In addition, that same pipeline ferries away refuse, exhaust gases, and worn-out chemicals. In the interest of economical transport, the body dissolves its vital substances into a liquid (much as coal is shipped more efficiently through a slurry pipeline than by truck or train). Five or six quarts of this all-purpose fluid suffice for the body's hundred trillion cells.[58]

After explaining the role of blood in bringing us life, Brand and Yancey state:

[E]very surgeon learns to identify blood with life. The two are inseparable; you lose one, you lose both.[59]

This explains the vitality of having blood in our physical bodies. Let's see how this helps us understand the way the life-giving blood of Christ nourishes our lives.

In John 6 Jesus said something that astounded His listeners:

Very truly I tell you, unless you eat the flesh of the Son of Man and drink his blood, you have no life in you. Whoever eats my flesh and drinks my blood has eternal life, and I will raise them up at the last day. For my flesh is real food and my blood is real drink. Whoever eats my flesh and drinks my blood remains in me, and I in them. Just as the living Father sent me and I live because of the Father, so the one who feeds on me will live because of me. (John 6:53–57, TNIV)

For His Jewish listeners, it was radical and contrary to the Law of Moses, which forbade the drinking of blood and the eating of meat with blood in it. Jesus was explaining the new covenant He brought not only to the Jews but also to the whole human race. Up to that time, the impact of the sprinkling of blood was imperfect and short-lived. It had to be repeated. Jesus showed that in the new covenant, the impact of His sacrifice was eternal. It was to change us from the inside out, so our behaviors express what's inside us (see Hebrews 9–10, Matthew 23,

Mark 7, Luke 11, and John 6). Again, I draw on Brand and Yancey's explanation:

> If I read these accounts correctly, they correspond to my medical experience exactly. *It is not true that blood represents life to the surgeon but death to the Christian. Rather we come to the table also to partake of His life.* "For my flesh is real food and my blood is real drink. Whoever eats my flesh and drinks my blood remains in me, and I in him"—at least those words make sense. Christ came not just to give us an example of a way of life but to give us life itself. Spiritual life is not ethereal and outside us, something that we must work hard to obtain; it is in us, pervading us, as blood is in every living being.[60]

Jesus instituted the Holy Communion (or Eucharist) not just to be exercised as a ritual at Christian gatherings but as a daily reminder—actually, every time we eat or drink—that we need to depend on His Spirit in us to cleanse and nourish us as we carry out our daily lives.

The blood of Christ through His Spirit is in all who receive Him. We can count on Christ to cleanse and nourish us daily and every minute and second of the day. Jesus illustrates this principle using the example of the vine and branches in John 15:

> *I am the vine; you are the branches. If you remain in me and I in you, you will bear much fruit; apart from me you can do nothing.* (John 15:5, TNIV)

As long as the branch remains connected to the vine, it draws nutrients from the vine. When it's cut off, it starts to die.

It may not be apparent at first, but as soon as a flower is cut from its stem, it starts dying. Any flower not attached to a plant soon withers. So it is with a person's spiritual life. Spirituality withers when a person isn't nourished through communion with Christ. I can think of no better way of connecting with God than through prayer and meditation on His words, the Bible.

Andrew Murray shows us how to drink the blood of Jesus:

> We speak sometimes of "drinking in" the words of a speaker, when we heartily give ourselves up to listen and receiving them. So when the heart of someone is filled with a sense of the preciousness and power of the blood; when he with real joy is lost in the contemplation of it; when he with wholehearted faith takes it for himself, and seeks to be convinced in his inner being the life-giving power of that blood; then it may be rightly said that he "drinks the blood of Jesus." All that faith enables him to see of redemption, of cleansing, of sanctification by the blood he absorbs into the depth of his soul.[61]

There are other, more mystical interpretations of drinking the blood of Jesus. Most are associated with interpreting the deeper meaning of the Last Supper and the Holy Communion. Much truth can be found in those interpretations, but we'll limit our discussion here. Through meditation on the Bible, practicing communion, and submission to the conviction of His Spirit in us through prayer, we receive Jesus into our hearts and minds, receiving cleansing and life-giving nourishment.

THE PARENT-FIRST VIEW: EXCHANGING POISON FOR POWER

This study reminds me of Jesus' words in Matthew 11:

> Come to me, all you who are weary and burdened, and I will give you rest. Take my yoke upon you and learn from me, for I am gentle and humble in heart, and you will find rest for your souls. For my yoke is easy and my burden is light. (Matthew 11:28–30, TNIV)

When I come to Jesus with my weariness and burdens, Jesus gives me rest in return.

All Christians have the Spirit of Christ. Ephesians 1:3 says,

[God] has blessed us in the heavenly realms with every spiritual blessing in Christ. (TNIV)

I have all I require to live a godly life. Unfortunately, I don't live a one hundred percent godly life. Each day as I interact with people, review my financial situation, worry about my vocational and business prospects, deal with my insecurities in relationships, or face whatever worldly challenges stand in my way, I'm affected by selfishness and worries, both mine and others'. In Brand and Yancey's words:

Pride, egotism, lust, and covetousness are simply poisons that interfere with our relationship to God and to other people. Sin results in separation between God and humanity, other people, and our true selves. The more we cling to our private desires, our thirst for success, our own satisfactions at the expense of others, the [further] we will drift from God and others.[62]

"Pride, egotism, lust, and covetousness are simply poisons that interfere with our relationship to God and to other people." —Paul Brand and Phillip Yancey

Jesus calls me to come to Him with whatever I've done wrong and surrender to Him my weariness and burdens, which come from sin. In exchange He gives me rest. I exchange the poison of my worldly pursuits for taking up His yoke. He teaches me to be gentle and humble like Him. My weariness turns to ease and my burden becomes light.

Physical blood cleanses the poison from my body and provides the energy and nourishment it requires. The blood of Christ cleanses sin from my life and nourishes me with His power and character to live in accordance with His will. Apostle Paul's teaching comes to mind:

Therefore, since we have been justified through faith, we have peace with God through our Lord Jesus Christ, through whom we have gained access by faith into this grace in which we now stand. And we boast in the hope of the glory of God. Not only so, but we also glory in our sufferings, because we know that suffering produces perseverance; perseverance, character; and character, hope. And hope does not put us to shame, because God's love has been poured out into our hearts through the Holy Spirit, who has been given to us. (Romans 5:1–5, TNIV)

The blood of Christ exhibits its power as the expression of love through the Holy Spirit, who has been given to us.

THE FORK IN THE ROAD

Life is all about loving relationships. As we go through life, our sins produce obstacles to love. Forgiveness removes these obstacles. Without forgiveness there is no love. Without love there is no life. When we read Hebrews 9:22, we can interpret it on the one hand to be about an immovable judge demanding that blood be shed as punishment before He is willing to forgive. On the other hand,

In Him we have redemption (deliverance and salvation) through His blood, the remission (forgiveness) of our offences (shortcomings and trespasses), in accordance with the riches and *the generosity of His gracious favor, which he lavished upon us.* (Ephesians 1:7–8, AMP)

Hebrews 9:22 teaches that the blood of Christ cleanses us from sin and gives us the grace and power we need to forgive and love, without associating it with punishment from God. Our interpretation of the shed blood of Christ in Hebrews 9:22 can lead us to the view of a judge-first God demanding punishment for sin. Alternatively, it can lead us to the view of a parent-first God offering relief from sin and life through Christ. I choose the view of the parent. What's your choice?

What About Christ's Death on the Cross?

Every thoughtful Christian asks this question, sooner or later: what about the death of Jesus on the cross? In other words, why did Jesus have to die?

THE TRADITIONAL JUDGE-FIRST VIEWS

Christians believe that Jesus is God in the flesh. When God Almighty chooses to live among us and allow His children to nail Him and leave Him to die on a cross, it's a universe-shattering event beyond comparison. Those who have given it thought can't help but try to understand why.

This question has been asked by Christians since the dawn of Christianity. During the two millennia of Christianity, theologians have proposed various explanations, called "atonement theories." In my research I identified at least twelve theories.[63] Although some claim they have exclusively correct interpretations, no proponent of one interpretation can realistically claim to have cornered the truth regarding the topic of the atonement.

> From the patristic period [the early church] onward, Christian theologians generally can be found acknowledging the rich

diversity of ways that the manifold aspects of the atonement can be expressed.[64]

This viewpoint, which promotes diversity rather than exclusivity in our understanding of God—within the boundaries of sound biblical interpretations, of course—is further illustrated by the four gospels. Some have tried to construct one gospel out of Matthew, Mark, Luke, and John, but Bible students increasingly regard each of the four gospels as a complete narrative of the life and ministry of Jesus Christ.

God inspired the writer of each gospel to show us a complete account of what Jesus Christ was like. It's similar to looking at four oil paintings of a famous person—for example, those of Winston Churchill. In one he may be wearing a military uniform; in another he may be in a business suit; in a third, a tuxedo; and in a fourth, casual clothing. Each portrait is correct and complete. No one can claim to be exclusively correct and exclude the others as invalid depictions.

It would be ridiculous to try to understand Winston Churchill through a composite picture wearing a tuxedo jacket with a military cap, casual trousers, and slippers. In the other extreme, some critics of the Bible have tried to strip out differences and boil the gospels down to their commonalities. This is also ridiculous. Imagine seeing Winston Churchill with only one eye and missing limbs, because some portraits show only the profile of his face or body.[65]

The same is true when we try to understand Christ's atonement. There have been many explanations for Christ's atonement over the centuries, because the Bible doesn't definitively explain *why* the death and resurrection of Christ bring reconciliation.

> *The Bible tells us in many ways what Christ has done for us. However, it doesn't explain why, other than it was achieved through Christ's life, death, and resurrection.*

The Bible talks about the atonement of Christ in many ways. In various English translations, we read that Christ Jesus, through His death and resurrection, ransomed us, died for our sins, bore our sins, saved us from our sins, forgave our sins, gave Himself for our sins, made purification of sins, made atonement (propitiation) for our sins, sacrificed for our sins, took away our sins, condemned sin, became sin, put away sin, and released or freed us from our sins. The Bible tells us in many ways *what* Christ has done for us. However, it doesn't explain *why*, other than that it was achieved through Christ's life, death, and resurrection.

Many modern-day Protestants—and evangelicals in particular—adopt a judge-first atonement theory.[66] They tend to believe this is the only way to explain why Jesus Christ died on the cross. The theory essentially teaches the following principles, which we've discussed in various earlier chapters:

1. All have sinned and fall short of God's perfect glory.
2. Because God is righteous and just, all sinners who fall short of God's perfection must be punished in accordance with divine retributive justice.
3. Because God is holy and pure, He cannot accept sinners in His presence. The punishment for sinners, therefore, is eternal separation from Him in hell.
4. God is also merciful and wants none to perish. That's why He came in the flesh through Jesus Christ, lived a sinless life, and on the cross took on the punishment all sinners deserve so that the requirements for divine retributive justice could be met.
5. Those who accept the death of Jesus on the cross as substitution and repent for their sins will be forgiven by God. God will accept them into His presence in eternity. God's perfect requirements for justice and mercy are met in those who receive this gift of salvation.
6. Others who haven't received this gift of salvation at the end of their earthly lives go to hell.

I know this is a clinical description, but it summarizes the theory. This theory is supported by the judge-first answers for the "What about…?" questions we've discussed. I have shown that the answers provided under the judge-first framework aren't exclusively right. There are biblically sound alternatives under the parent-first framework.

LET'S DIG MORE DEEPLY

In view of the many atonement theories and the passion by which Christians have discussed this topic since the early days of Christianity, it becomes clear that many want to understand why Jesus went to the cross. This is important, especially for those who are interested in sharing their faith with others. In 1 Peter 3:15, the Bible tells us to "be prepared to give an answer to everyone who asks you to give the reason for the hope that you have." Since the life, death, and resurrection of Christ are at the center of the Christian faith, how we explain the atonement of Christ matters.

The life, death, and resurrection of Jesus Christ are inseparable. God incarnates as Jesus to live among us on earth. Without His life on earth, there is no death on the cross. Without death on the cross, there is no resurrection. Without resurrection, the life of Christ brings no eternal fruit, and His death brings no hope for the future. God came in the flesh through Jesus precisely so that He could live and go to the cross. Jesus was the Lamb of God precisely so that He could take away our sin (John 2:29). Jesus lay down His life on the cross precisely so that He could take it up again (John 10:17–18). The Lamb was slain and rose again precisely so that He could stand victorious in the center of the throne in heaven (Revelation 5:6).

> *The life, death, and resurrection of Jesus Christ are inseparable.*

Jesus as Lamb of God is based on the concept of the sacrificial lamb that brought reconciliation between God and the faithful Jew. The sacrificial lamb is deeply embedded in the Old Testament as a remembrance of the Israelites' deliverance from the angel of death and slavery in Egypt. It's also an offering through which the faithful reconcile with God. Jesus as the Lamb of God rescues humankind from condemnation and slavery of sin, reconciling sinners with God through His death. The biblical view of the sacrificial lamb, therefore, is deliverance and rescue.

The lambs in the Old Testament offerings died and remained dead. The sacrificial lambs brought forgiveness for the past but no hope for the future. That's why the offerings had to be repeated:

Every priest stands daily ministering and offering time after time the same sacrifices. (Hebrews 10:11, NASB)

In contrast, Jesus offers Himself up once and for all, providing eternal hope for the faithful because of His victorious resurrection from death. In Hebrews 10:12, we read,

But He, having offered one sacrifice for sins for all time, sat down at the right hand of God. (NASB)

Jesus was slain and then raised by the resurrection power of the Holy Spirit so that the Lamb of God could be victorious on the throne (Revelation 5:6). The Lamb of God, as the resurrected Christ, assures eternal hope for all creation in addition to forgiveness of sins.

The same Spirit who raised the Lamb from the dead is in the life of all believers so that through the resurrection power of the Holy Spirit they can also conquer sin and sin's consequences (see 1 Corinthians 6:14, Ephesians 1:19–20). Through His sacrifice the Lamb of God secures humankind's forgiveness. Through the power of the resurrection, the Spirit secures eternal hope for all from now to eternity.

When we receive Christ, in addition to receiving the forgiveness that results from Christ's sacrifice, we also receive the Spirit of Christ into our lives. The indwelling Spirit of Christ is the same Spirit who resurrected Jesus from death and overcame the power of sin. This same power is available to all Christians to gain victory over temptation and sin when they submit to the inner conviction of sin and gain the freedom to obey.

THE ROMAN ROAD, REVISITED

In summary, here's how Jesus Christ brings humankind to be reconciled with God:

1. Roman 3:23: "For all have sinned and fall short of the glory of God." We tend to love ourselves more than we love others or God. As a result we often do what pleases us, disobeying God at the expense of others. This is what the Bible calls sin. All humans sin. In our sin we

turn away from God in this life and eternity. This has been true since the first humans, Adam and Eve.

2. Romans 6:23a: "For the wages of sin is death…" When we sin we hurt ourselves, other people, and fall short of the life of love God desires for us. Our sin causes self-protection, broken relationships, hatred, bloodshed, betrayal, and numerous ugly consequences beyond our understanding and control. The Bible calls these consequences "the wages of sin."

3. Romans 6:23b: "…but the gift of God is eternal life in Christ Jesus our Lord." God is merciful and is committed to rescue us from our sin. He came in the flesh through Jesus Christ and lived a sinless life. As the Lamb of God, Jesus Christ died on the cross and suffered the totality of all the wages of our sin. Through this act of sacrifice, Jesus absorbed and removed the burden of sin for all humankind.

4. Romans 10:9: "That if you confess with your mouth, 'Jesus is Lord,' and believe in your heart that God raised him from the dead, you will be saved." After Jesus suffered death as the consequence of our sin, He rose from the dead through the power of the Holy Spirit, declaring victory over sin and all its ugly consequences, including death. When we believe what Jesus has done for us and put our trust in Him, we become God's children and receive God's forgiveness and His Spirit, who gives us the power to save us from our sin and follow God's way of love. We make a U-turn away from a life of selfish pursuits, toward a way of love and fellowship with God and other children of God.

THE PARENT-FIRST VIEW

This parent-first explanation shows God's loving, graceful, wide-ranging, powerful, and spare-no-effort initiative in His incarnation through Christ as the Lamb of God to rescue humankind from sin:

> *For he chose us in him before the creation of the world to be holy and blameless in his sight. In love he predestined us for adoption to sonship through Jesus Christ.…In him we have redemption through his blood, the forgiveness of sins, in accordance with the riches of God's grace that he lavished on us.* (Ephesians 1:4–5, 7–8, TNIV)

God had in mind this plan of redemption before the world existed. Through Christ, God redeems and forgives us.

Jesus Christ received the deadly consequences on our behalf. The source of Christ's suffering is our sin and its ugly consequences, *not* punishment from God.

[God] made Him who knew no sin to be sin on our behalf, so that we might become the righteousness of God in Him. (2 Corinthians 5:21, NASB)

Christ brought us righteousness by being made sin and taking on all the ugliness and wages of sin on our behalf, relieving us of the burden of sin.

WHY THE PARENT-FIRST EXPLANATION IS IMPORTANT

Traditionally, a major obstacle preventing people from accepting Christianity is its portrayal of a God who demands violence as payment for sins. Greg Boyd asks:

If God must always get what is coming to him in order to forgive (namely, "a kill"), does God ever really forgive?[67]

> *A parent-first explanation of the gospel of Jesus Christ resolves many criticisms from the unchurched toward Christianity.*

In other words, if God demands payment of some sort, especially something as severe as death, how real is this forgiveness? If I demand punishment equivalent to or even more severe than the harm done, there's no meaning or worth to my so-called forgiveness.

The parent-first explanation avoids this criticism by putting the source of the wages of sin on sinners, not on God. God doesn't demand death as payment for sin. We bring death through our sin.

Many are skeptical of Christianity because it appears to them that God paints Himself into a corner by demanding equal satisfaction of both retributive justice and mercy. Many Christians have described this as God's dilemma; the only solution is to suffer the consequence of God's own demands for retributive justice through Christ, thereby satisfying mercy by relieving sinners of their inevitable retribution from God.

We are all familiar with the story Jesus told of the lost son in Luke 15:11–32. After losing his entire fortune through wasteful living, the lost son wanted to return home, even if just as a servant. When he approached home, the father saw him at a distance, had compassion, ran to him, embraced him, and kissed him. He interrupted his son's prepared confession and unconditionally welcomed him home with a big party (Luke 15:20–24).

However, the judge-first way of explaining how sinners can come home to God actually goes something like this. When the son approached home, the father said to him, "Look, I must maintain justice and fairness. Your sins must be punished in order to fulfill my requirement for righteousness. But I am also merciful and loving. I and your firstborn brother decided to let your firstborn brother be punished and banished in your place. If you accept His sacrifice as substitution for your well-deserved punishment, all is forgiven. Welcome home! If you don't accept, then you can go back to your pigsty and I never want to see you again."

Many people find it difficult to understand: if God sets all the rules, why would He demand contradictory requirements of both retributive justice and mercy? However, since the parent-first explanation proposes divine *restorative* justice, which fulfills the requirements of mercy, there is no dilemma. *Restorative justice is merciful, and it is merciful to administer restorative justice. They complement each other.*

A parent-first explanation of the gospel of Jesus Christ resolves many criticisms from the unchurched toward Christianity. Often, Christians take a defensive posture and fail to address these questions to inquirers' satisfaction. We often ask inquirers to suspend their reasoning and accept our explanation of a Father as Judge and a Son as Savior "in faith." Although no one can ever fully understand God's ways, our faith shouldn't cause us to consider questions we can't answer as illegitimate.

But in your hearts set apart Christ as Lord. Always be prepared to give an answer to everyone who asks you to give the reason for the hope that you have. But do this with gentleness and respect. (1 Peter 3:15)

The fact that our theological framework doesn't provide answers that make sense to the seeker doesn't mean the questions are unreasonable. The parent-first explanation provides answers to these questions. The punishment Jesus takes on comes not from a God who demands payment for our sin; the source of the punishment is the deadly consequences of our sin. God is given all the glory for our redemption through the gracious expression of His restorative justice and mercy. This view doesn't depict an immovable judge who has to resolve the dilemma between retributive justice and mercy, but a relentlessly loving parent who redeems His lost children at infinite cost to Himself and offers merciful restorative justice.

OUR FINAL FORK IN THE ROAD

This has been a long journey for my wife and me, one that has taken more than ten years. It started with a common question among Christians about those who had never heard of Jesus Christ. When we found what we thought was the right answer, it didn't fit with the framework we had been taught, leading us to ask more questions. Seeking answers to these questions sent us on a journey to experience more of God's relentless parental love.

For us the "Aha!" moment came when we understood the difference between the view of an immovable *judge* administering inflexible retributive justice and the view of a relentlessly loving *parent* administering restorative justice. As we applied the parent-first view in answering the "What about...?" questions, we saw with increasing clarity a parent who would stop at absolutely nothing, including allowing His children to crucify Him on the cross, to bring restoration and reconciliation to His creation and beloved children.

So, at the final fork on the road, we once again choose between two paths. The judge-first explanation of the crucifixion shows God sacrificing Himself through Christ, taking on God's punishment for humankind's sins before He can offer forgiveness for those who accept the substitution. The parent-first explanation shows God bearing in Christ our sin and all its ugly consequences which we cause so we can receive remission from sin and be reconciled with God and one another. Then, through the power of the resurrected Christ, God offers victorious life to those who receive Him.

The follow diagram summarizes the how the choices we make along the way lead us to the heart of a loving parent.

What are your choices?

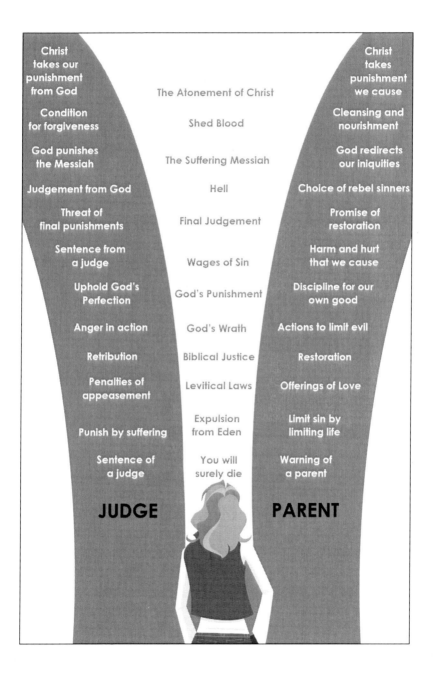

JUDGE		PARENT
Christ takes our punishment from God	The Atonement of Christ	Christ takes punishment we cause
Condition for forgiveness	Shed Blood	Cleansing and nourishment
God punishes the Messiah	The Suffering Messiah	God redirects our iniquities
Judgement from God	Hell	Choice of rebel sinners
Threat of final punishments	Final Judgement	Promise of restoration
Sentence from a judge	Wages of Sin	Harm and hurt that we cause
Uphold God's Perfection	God's Punishment	Discipline for our own good
Anger in action	God's Wrath	Actions to limit evil
Retribution	Biblical Justice	Restoration
Penalties of appeasement	Levitical Laws	Offerings of Love
Punish by suffering	Expulsion from Eden	Limit sin by limiting life
Sentence of a judge	You will surely die	Warning of a parent

So What?

FOURTEEN

JUDGE OR FATHER?

"Every day when I get home, I ask for God's forgiveness," said a prostitute in a CNN interview. When I heard that, I burst into tears. I was watching a special about the impact of an oppressive dictatorship that had bankrupted a resource-rich African country and how the people coped. This woman had been a hairdresser. When the area she was living in was bulldozed because of harsh and discriminatory government policies and corruption, her livelihood disintegrated. With twelve family members to support, she sold the only thing she possessed that people would pay for—her body. She gave up her dignity and risked her life, since the chance of her encountering violence and contracting HIV/AIDS was extremely high. All she wanted was to house, clothe, and feed her family. It was a noble act of sacrifice. I found it incredibly sad that her view of God resulted in fear of His judgment instead of hope for comfort and strength from God, her Father in heaven.

We start our most famous Christian prayer with "Our Father in heaven…." A loving father would be heartbroken to see His child resort to prostitution to gain income to care for her family. A loving father would love to hold her in his arms and comfort her. After sacrificing herself every day, why would this young woman feel she needed God's forgiveness? What prevented her from seeking instead God's comfort, strength, and guidance to endure another sexual assault?

The answer is simple: the prevalent judge-first view of God. This view causes such a person to seek God's forgiveness for giving up all she has for the sake of others. Granted, everyone benefits from God's forgiveness, but had this woman realized that God was for her and not against her, would she have turned to God as a parent for comfort and strength and not as a judge from whom she would need forgiveness? Whether a different view of God would have changed her economic situation, I don't know. Perhaps, with a more positive mindset, she might have been able to see a safer and more socially acceptable way of making a living. Perhaps not. But I believe having God as her Father in heaven would have allowed her to endure her suffering with the comfort of God's presence and not the fear of God's judgment.

WHO SHOULD JUDGE?

> *The judge-first view of God has almost nothing to do with the father of the prodigal son Jesus describes.*

The judge-first view of God has almost nothing to do with the father of the prodigal son Jesus describes. In His day Jesus was accused by the religious leaders for being a friend of sinners (Matthews 11:19, Luke 7:34). This is an "honor" that few present-day Christians enjoy. In *What's So Amazing About Grace?*, Philip Yancey opens with a story about a prostitute who "rented" out her two-year-old daughter for kinky sex acts to make money to feed her drug habit. She was shocked at the suggestion of turning to a church for help. Yancey observes:

> The woman much like this prostitute fled toward Jesus, not away from Him. The worse a person felt about herself, the more likely she saw Jesus as a refuge. Has the church lost that gift? Evidently the down-and-out, who flocked to Jesus when

he lived on earth, no longer feel welcome among his followers. What has happened?[68]

There may be many contributing factors. I believe our traditional view of a judge-first God has a lot to do with how we relate to other people, Christians and otherwise. Although it's true the Bible teaches that all have sinned, the question is whether it is up to us to judge and convict other people of their sinfulness.

Evangelical Christians are known for their desire to share their faith. When we share our faith according to the widely accepted judge-first atonement theory, we have to first convince others that they're sinners deserving of God's punishment. Although this paves the way to explain how God also shows His love for us by punishing Jesus, the Son of God, this explanation is based on the narrow understanding that God must maintain retributive justice by punishing each and every sinner for each and every sinful act. As a result, many Christians expend a tremendous amount of energy to prove that people are deserving of God's punishment. We can't get away from it, because until we convince others that God as judge must punish them for their sins, we have no way of explaining why Jesus had to die for them.

GOOD NEWS ANSWERS FOR THE TOUGH QUESTIONS

We face some common questions when we share our faith. Often, we feel that the questions are based on people's reluctance to receive what we call "good news." It's difficult, however, to tell people about a judge who's bent on punishing them for any and all things they do that fail to measure up to God's perfection. How can we call that "good news"? It is, indeed, good news that we have Jesus Christ as Savior, but we have to take others through the bad news about the judge first. It's confusing to accept that God the Father and God the Son are one while their characters appear to be opposite.

The traditional doctrine forces us to first explain to people the bad news that God must punish us before we can explain the saving grace of Jesus Christ. This explanation is unnecessary because the real bad new is our sin and its ugly consequences, not God's eternal punishment. Most people recognize the consequences of sin in their lives. We can be the source—and also the recipient—of these consequences. Our sin is bad news, indeed. When it comes to God, however, it's good news all the way because of the loving parent who gives Himself totally through the ministry of Jesus Christ, the suffering Messiah.

With this understanding we can provide biblically sound good news answers to the difficult questions we discussed in Chapter Eight.

Question: So, God became a human and punished Himself according to His own rules so He could forgive us?

Answer: God doesn't have a rule that He must punish each and every sin in each and every sinner. When we sin we bring negative consequences that hurt ourselves, people around us, our environment, and God. These consequences are what we call the wages of sin. God the Father became human in Christ to take on the wages of sin we impose on one another and Him, releasing us from sin so we can receive and give forgiveness.

Question: This seems more like schizophrenia than justice and love to me, don't you think?

Answer: It isn't schizophrenia when a perfectly loving parent gives totally of Himself, including death on a cross, to rescue His children from death. It's perfect love expressed through perfect mercy and restorative justice.

Question: I didn't ask to be born, you know. How can I trust a God who let me be born imperfect and then punishes me when He knows I can't help but be imperfect?

Answer: It's true that we can't help but fall short of perfection, and our sin causes harm and the death of loving relationships. But God doesn't insist on punishing us. He does want us to learn to love perfectly. When we confess, God forgives us and gives us everything we need to live in accordance with His love. We can make a U-turn from going the wrong way and start moving in the right direction of perfect love for the rest of our lives. That's good news.

Question: You mean God the Son died to save us from God the Father?

Answer: God the Son is God the Father in human flesh. He died to save us from the consequences of our sins. God the Son saves us not from the Father but from our own sins and their consequences, now and in eternity.

Here's the bottom line: God suffers through Christ and takes on all the bad news we cause through our sin so that when we hear about and receive His offer of forgiveness and new life, it's good news all the way, from start to finish.

HOW WE CAN SHARE THE GOOD NEWS

With this understanding of the good news, we can review how to share the good news with others. There are three outcomes we can share with friends who are interested in relating to God in a loving relationship.

First, Jesus, the suffering Messiah, took upon Himself on the cross all the penalties we have caused others. Trevor Seath, my friend and pastor, once wrote to me:

The Almighty God, as Jesus, endured by choice what we, by choice, had inflicted upon ourselves. We pulled the trigger and Jesus took the bullet. We stepped off the edge and Jesus took the fall. We overdosed and Jesus flatlined. We committed suicide by rejecting the Source of life, and Jesus volunteered to die our death. Death was the consequence of our situation and Jesus voluntarily took that consequence upon Himself.

Jesus has taken all the pain and hurt that we've caused. At the final judgment, He'll restore the losses and heal all harms we've imposed on others. Because of this, *we have the freedom to ask others to forgive us.*

149

Second, since Jesus has also taken the losses and pains others have caused us, we can count on Him to restore and heal us from our losses and pains. Therefore, we have the freedom to forgive others who have sinned against us. We can look to God's promise to bring restorative justice to our lives, if not now then in eternity. We don't need to hold onto the anger and bitterness caused by other people's offense against us. We're free to forgive.

Third, and most important, God has also forgiven us. God has shown us that death is the essential outcome of our sin. We read in Hebrews,

> *But we do see Jesus, who was made lower than the angels for a little while, now crowned with glory and honor because he suffered death, so that by the grace of God he might taste death for everyone.* (Hebrews 2:9, TNIV)

Jesus suffered the consequences of our sin and offered us forgiveness. While on the cross, Jesus said,

> *Father, forgive them, for they do not know what they are doing.* (Luke 23:34, TNIV)

> *Each of us has the freedom to seek forgiveness from others we've hurt, can forgive others who have hurt us, and can receive God's forgiveness… That's good news, indeed!*

We can trust that God answers the prayers of Christ. When we receive God's forgiveness, we have the freedom *and obligation* to forgive others (see Matthew 6:12-14, Luke 6:37, and Colossians 3:13).

Consider this. Each of us has the freedom to seek forgiveness from others we've hurt, can forgive others who have hurt us, and can receive God's forgiveness. Now, if every human being comes to this realization, that's good news, indeed!

Evangelism based on the parent-first explanation removes common objections to trusting Christ for eternity based on traditional judge-first interpretations. This explanation shows a God who spares no effort to redeem His children from sin and death without first imposing on them the death penalty. Adopting this view may direct believers to focus on helping unchurched friends encounter and experience a God who's consistent with the compassionate and forgiving father of the Prodigal Son in Luke 15:11–32. In this famous story about God, there's no trace of condemnation from the father to the sinful son. Perhaps Jesus, who uses this story to tell us about God, wants His followers to share their faith in the same way.

In an e-mail exchange with Christopher Marshall, author of *Beyond Retribution* and a leader in biblical justice, he wrote:

> I often say to students, "Imagine if God really is like the father of the prodigal son." I believe he is—because I trust Jesus' judgment on such things. And if he is, that settles the question of what kind of justice he shows—it is compassionate justice!

Our interpretation of Christ's atonement can have an impact on our understanding of how God relates to us and how we ought to relate to one another. The judge-first atonement theory requires a God who's an immovable judge, enforcing inflexible retributive justice by imposing eternal damnation as punishment on all sinners. This may provide a basis for explaining why Jesus had to die, but such a view has a profound impact on how we relate to God and people, and how we share our faith. If I want to convince others to put their trust in Christ based on this traditional interpretation, it would be necessary for me to convince them *first* that God the judge insists on punishing them for their sins through eternal damnation. This is counterintuitive to the teaching of a loving God and contrary to how humans believe an emotionally healthy parent should act.

Further, I feel that those who hold a view of God the Father as an immovable judge tend to be judgmental. North American Christians, and evangelicals in particular, are widely regarded by the unchurched as some of the most rigid, bigoted, and judgmental people in society. I feel that our views of God as an immovable judge may have had an impact on our attitudes toward others, causing us to be more judgmental than

God intends us to be. Relating to God as a loving parent may help some to be more accepting, loving, and generous.

Let's see how a conversation with a seeker might take place if we were to share our faith in a parent-first God.

Simon the Seeker: Why should I become a Christian?

Chris the Christian: Humans are imperfect and we've all done something wrong. Even when we love someone deeply, we inevitably do something to hurt them. That's why the Bible tells us that "all have sinned." When we sin we usually hurt others and even ourselves. Sometimes we can make amends, but other times there are hurts we can't patch up, no matter how much we want to. Can you relate to that?

Simon: Yeah. I know I'm not perfect. I admit that sometimes I just can't help but lash out in anger or anxiety, saying or doing things I wish I could have retrieved or undone, but I can't. But I've never meant to hurt anyone. Sometimes I hurt people without even knowing it.

Chris: I know what you mean. The hurt and harm we cause when we sin is what the Bible calls "the wages of sin." It's not good news. The good news is that God loves us and wants to help us overcome our tendency to sin, relieving us of the consequences of our sin through Jesus Christ.

Simon: How does He do that?

Chris: In order to help us relate to Him, God became a man through Jesus Christ. It's like if we would want to relate to the ants in an ant colony; the most effective way would be to become an ant and communicate at their level. So, God stuffed Himself into a human body through Jesus Christ. That's why Jesus is called the Son of God. It doesn't mean Jesus was inferior to God; it means Jesus had within Him all of God. Being perfect, Jesus Christ never sinned. In addition to teaching about God and demonstrating the love of God when He was on the earth, Jesus' mission was to take on the cross all the ugly consequences of humankind's sin. When He died on the cross, the Bible tells us that He became sin and absorbed into Himself all the wages of our sins so that He could offer us forgiveness.

Simon: I don't get it.

Chris: When we sin, the consequences often result in losses for others—and even for ourselves, right?

Simon: Right.

Chris: What if God tells us that He'll restore all the losses we cause? When we know that all the losses others cause us will be restored someday, it helps us forgive others. In fact, since God is our Father in heaven, we also offend Him when we sin. Through Christ, God offers His forgiveness for our sin. When God forgives us, He also expects us to forgive others. Jesus is worthy of doing this because He personally took on the sinful losses of all humankind. Will that help us receive God's forgiveness and forgive one another for the harm we cause?

Simon: If indeed God can and will restore all the losses I cause others, and all the losses others cause me, it's good news all right.

Chris: The good news doesn't stop there. Jesus didn't stay dead. Sin couldn't keep Him down. God used His power to raise Jesus Christ from the dead, showing His power over sin and sin's deadly consequences. This resurrection power comes from the Holy Spirit. You see, not only do we need forgiveness from sin, we also need the power to change so we can learn to stop sinning and hurting other people, ourselves, and God. When we put our trust in Jesus Christ, God offers us His Spirit so we can start a new life, following Jesus Christ.

Simon: What do you mean by putting our trust in Jesus Christ?

Chris: God doesn't thrust His love and forgiveness down our throats. We can receive this gift by believing that Jesus Christ has won the victory over sin and its ugly consequences through His resurrection from the dead, and that He can come into our lives through His Spirit to give us the power to start a new life of love and victory over sin. Anyone can receive that by simply asking. Is this something you want to do?

Simon: Hook me up, dude!

Epilogue

This book has been in the making since 2003. On the one hand, it's immensely gratifying to have finally documented and communicated this journey and its delightful discoveries under a biblically coherent framework. It is now possible to complete those previously frustrating and inconclusive dialogues that began with "What about…?" questions.

God's goal is to reconcile His creation back to *shalom* through Christ so that all creation exists in relational peace: people with people, people with all creation, and the most important of all, people with God. Our sins bring death. Christ paid the wages of our sins in His death and brought life through His resurrection.

I hope you're excited and encouraged to rediscover the Almighty God who chooses to relate to us as the gentle, humble, and waiting Parent, the perfect and victorious Lamb, and the powerful indwelling Spirit. This intense and fulfilling journey has required my wife and me to reexamine many doctrines that were taught to us as exclusive truths by well-meaning teachers. For someone who was steeped in the teaching of the judge-first view of God for the first twenty-three years of Christian life, it was challenging—and at times scary—for me to explore these unfamiliar paths.

Above all, it has been an exhilarating journey through which we can discover and experience the relentless parental love of God more each day.

I encourage you to continue this wonderful journey on your own. I hope you can start studying the word of God though glasses with a different tint—the tint of a relentlessly loving parent administering restorative justice.

Our belief on how God relates to us through Christ has a significant impact on how we live out our faith. Evangelism would be more effective if Christians adopted a biblically sound and parent-first perspective of God, removing some of the stigmas and seeming contradictions that exist between a punishing Father and a saving Son.

From personal observation, it seems that it's easier for someone to rebel against a stern judge than against a loving parent. Something inside us responds more positively to love than to judgment. I often wonder whether it's easier for a wayward child to return to the warm embrace of a loving and waiting parent who is watching for the child's return and restoration, than to return to face a stern judge who insists that some retributive consequences must be dealt with before forgiveness can be offered.

Many people around us are alienated from God. If those who are living apart from God get to know their relentlessly loving and waiting Father, I wonder whether more would gladly turn to His embrace. I know that sharing redemption through Christ using the parent-first explanation has been better received by the unchurched than using the traditional judge-first explanation. If all Christians could allow this relentless parental love to work through them to touch people, more people will turn to Christ.

Endnotes

1 Chris Eaton and Amy Grant, *Out in The Open*, Simple Things (Warner/Chappell Music, Inc., Los Angeles, CA).

2 Explanations for the sacrifice of Jesus Christ are called atonement theories. There are many of them, but one in particular—penal substitution—is the most commonly accepted among evangelicals; it's usually considered to be the only valid one.

3 It would be necessary for Jesus Christ to have lived a sinless life, otherwise he'd have to take the punishment of death for His own sins. If Jesus had to die for His own sins, His death would be ineffective in paying for someone else's sins.

4 I know the Kidz Camp's operation quite intimately because my son took over from Scott as director for several years and continued to attract more children each year. During that time he built wonderful relationships with the children and their parents. However, he never felt comfortable asking the children to pray the sinner's prayer.

5 Dallas Willard. *The Divine Conspiracy* (New York, NY: Harper Collins, 1999), pp. 36–37.

6 Oswald Chambers. *My Utmost for His Highest, Updated Edition* (Grand Rapid, MI: Discovery House Publishers, 2012), April 29 entry.

7 Richard Rodgers and Oscar Hammerstein, *Do-Re-Me*, Sound of Music (Hal Leonard, HL.312394).

8 *New Commentary on the Whole Bible: Old Testament Volume* (Wheaton, IL: Tyndale House Publications, 1990). Electronic Edition, Genesis 2:17.

9 Oswald Chambers. *My Utmost for His Highest Updated Edition* (Grand Rapids, MI: Discovery House Publishers, 2012), June 23 entry.

10 Ephesians 1:4 (TNIV): "For he chose us in him *before the creation of the world* to be holy and blameless in his sight" (emphasis added).

11 Romans 5:8 (TNIV): "But God demonstrates his own love for us in this: While we were still sinners, Christ died for us."

12 How do children learn to lie? No sane parents teach their children to lie. But somehow, without anyone teaching them, the tendency of young children who can barely talk is to lie when they feel they've done something wrong. It's a mystery, from a logical perspective. From a biblical perspective, however, we can see that children simply carry on what Adam and Eve started in Genesis 3. Parents have to teach their children *not* to lie.

13 Philip Yancey. *Rumors of Another World* (Grand Rapids, MI: Zondervan, 2003), p. 185.

14 Matthew 5:27–30: "You have heard that it was said, 'Do not commit adultery.' But I tell you that anyone who looks at a woman lustfully has already committed adultery with her in his heart. If your right eye causes you to sin, gouge it out and throw it away. It is better for you to lose one part of your body than for your whole body to be thrown into hell. And if your right hand causes you to sin, cut it off and throw it away. It is better for you to lose one part of your body than for your whole body to go into hell."

15 I recently heard a sermon that represented this viewpoint. The preacher tried to explain why there's a command in Genesis 2 from God for Adam and Eve to avoid eating the fruit from the Tree of the Knowledge of Good and Evil. There was no other rule in Eden. However, Adam and Eve were unable to keep even that one command, proving that humans were incapable of being obedient. This was the reason, according to the preacher, for the existence of the Tree of the Knowledge of Good and Evil.

16 All translations from one language to another are necessarily interpretations. Often there are no word-for-word matches, forcing the translators to interpret the meaning of the source text and choose the closest approximation in the target language. Biases and cultures often color the outcome of the translation/interpretation process.

17 Shalom means peace, but not merely the absence of war-- shalom means a deep sort of peace in which everything is right and good. It's a Hebrew word from the Old Testament. http://www.webanswers.com/social-sciences/spiritual-religious/judaism-torah/what-does-shalome-mean-587b53 (Retrieved on February 2, 2013).

18 Romans 7:13 talks about this utter sinfulness: "But sin, that it might appear sin, was producing death in me through what is good, so that sin through the commandment might become exceedingly sinful" (NKJV).

19 This is about the same as "a tenth of an ephah" (Leviticus 5:11).

20 The Holman Bible Dictionary, Electronic Edition (Nashville, TN: Holman Bible Publishers, 2001).

21 Christopher Marshall. *The Little Book of Biblical Justice* (Intercourse, PA: Good Books, 2005), p. 11.

22 CBC News. "Bail denied for U.S. man jailed for consensual teen sex." Date of retrieval: July 4, 2007 (http://www.cbc.ca/world/story/2007/06/27/teen-sex-case.html).

23 Ibid.

24 CBC News. "Paris liberated: celebutante completes jail term." Date of retrieval: July 4, 2007 (http://www.cbc.ca/arts/media/story/2007/06/26/free-paris.html).

25 Joel B. Green & Mark D. Baker. *Recovering the Scandal of the Cross* (Downers Grove, IL: InterVarsity Press, 2000), pp. 24–25.

26 Christopher Marshall. *Beyond Retribution* (Grand Rapids, MI: Wm. B. Eerdmans Publishing Co., 2001), p. 48.

27 Ibid., p. 47.

28 Jerry Bridges. *The Gospel for Real Life* (Colorado Springs, CO: NavPress, 2002), p. 43. Emphasis added.

29 CBC News. "Special Report: Famine in Africa." Date of retrieval: September 24, 2011 (http://www.cbc.ca/news/world/story/2011/07/20/f-africa-famine-topix.html).

30 Dictionary.com. "Wrath." Date of retrieval: February 3, 2007 (http://dictionary.reference.com/browse/wrath).

31 Blue Letter Bible. "Strong's G3709–*orgē*." Date of retrieval: December 2, 2012 (http://www.blueletterbible.org/lang/lexicon/lexicon.cfm?strongs=G3709).

32 Max Lucado. *Experiencing the Heart of Jesus* (Nashville, TN: Thomas Nelson, 2004), p. 49.

33 This may open another can of doctrinal worms about God's sovereignty and humanity's free will, an argument that has raged for millennia without resolution. This topic is definitely beyond the scope of this book. It's fair to say, however, that my specific doctrinal preference notwithstanding, humanity does appear to have freedom of choice—at least from our earthly perspective. Ask yourself, if God didn't stop Adam or Eve from sinning, why would He stop anyone else?

34 For example, death by crucifixion was a common form of Roman punishment. One can scarcely get more retributive than that.

35 Note that the absence of a word in scripture doesn't mean that the concept is absent. However, the differences are so overwhelming that there's little doubt the NLT translation uses words with more retributive overtones than the other two versions.

36 There are many more *p* words in the OT than in the NT; it may imply a more punitive view of God in the OT than in the NT. However, a more careful reading will show that most of the punishments in the OT are in the disciplinary context and eternal punishment is not mentioned.

37 According to Genesis 3:22–24, the purpose of the expulsion was to prevent access to the tree of life: "Then the Lord God said, 'Behold, the man has become like one of Us, to know good and evil. And now, *lest he put out his hand and take also of the tree of life, and eat, and live forever'—therefore the Lord God sent him out of the garden of Eden to till the ground from which he was taken.* So He drove out the man; and He placed cherubim at the east of the garden of Eden, and a flaming sword which turned every way, to guard the way to the tree of life" (NKJV, emphasis added).

38 We don't know whether the father was alive, but we can assume it was not the church member's birth mother.

39 *Adam Clarke's Commentary on the New Testament*, Electronic Edition STEP Files, QuickVerse 7, 1999, Parsons Technology, Inc.

40 At the last revision of this book, David has gone through another loop. He was arrested for robbery, tried, and spent six months in jail. He got out, stayed clean for about five months, relapsed, and was caught by police in a stolen car. He is again back in jail. We continue to be his friends and pray for him.

41 "All of us have become like one who is unclean, and all our righteous acts are like filthy rags; we all shrivel up like a leaf, and like the wind our sins sweep us away" (Isaiah 64:6, TNIV).

42 999jokes.com. "An elderly lady was well-known for her faith…" Date of retrieval: September 10, 2011 (http://www.9999jokes.com/jokes/an-elderly-lady-was-well-known-for-her-faith-and-for-her-boldness-in-talking-about-it-she-woul).

43 Joel B. Green & Mark D. Baker. *Recovering the Scandal of the Cross* (Downers Grove, IL: InterVarsity Press, 2000), p. 21.

44 Amazon.com. "Love Wins: A Book About Heaven, Hell, and the Fate of Every Person Who Ever Lived." Date of retrieval: June 1, 2012 (http://www.amazon.com/Love-Wins-About-Heaven-Person/dp/0062049658/ref=sr_1_1?ie=UTF8&qid=1348715770&sr=8-1&keywords=Love+Wins).

45 Christopher Marshall. *Beyond Retribution* (Grand Rapids, MI: Wm. B. Eerdmans Publishing Co., 2001), pp. 197–198.

46 The references are too many to list exhaustively. Those who are interested can refer to Matthew 10:15, 2 Peter 2:9, 1 John 2:17, and Revelation 20:11–15.

47 Timothy Keller. *The Reason for God* (New York, NY: Riverhead Books, 2009), p. 71.

48 This is similar to Buddhism's afterlife concept. In Buddhism, however, it's a punishment for a soul to be reincarnated for another life of suffering but a reward to achieve nirvana (nothingness), like a drop of water returning to the ocean, erasing all sense of self, thus setting the soul at rest.

49 Some confuse universalism with agnosticism, which teaches that no one knows for sure how to reach God. Universalism is also different from pantheism, which teaches that all ways lead to God. Christian universalism embraces Christ alone as the Way to reconcile with God and that this reconciliation applies to all humankind regardless of earthly religiosity.

50 Anvari.org. "A man arrives at the gates of heaven. St. Peter asks, 'Religion?'" Date of retrieval: December 2, 2012 (http://www.anvari.org/shortjoke/St_Peter/222_a-man-arrives-at-the-gates-of-heaven-st-peter-asks-religion.html). Modified to fit the context.

51 C.S. Lewis. *The Great Divorce* (New York, NY: HarperCollins, 1973), p. 75.

52 Timothy Keller. *The Reason for God* (New York, NY: Riverhead Books, 2009), pp. 79–82.

53 The word *remission* (Strong's G859) is normally related as "forgiveness." However, the Greek word also means "release from bondage." These definitions lead to questions about whether Hebrews 9:22 refers to forgiveness from people or God or simply release from the bondage of sin.

54 Various Authors. *The Incredible Machine* (Washington, DC: The National Geographic Society, 1996), p. 99. Chapter Four, "The Powerful River," contributed by Susan Schiefelbein.

55 Paul Brand and Phillip Yancey. *In His Image* (Grand Rapids, MI: Zondervan, 1984), pp. 74–75.

56 Various Authors. *The Incredible Machine* (Washington, DC: The National Geographic Society, 1996), p. 99. Chapter Four, "The Powerful River," contributed by Susan Schiefelbein.

57 Ibid.

58 Paul Brand and Phillip Yancey. *In His Image* (Grand Rapids, MI: Zondervan, 1984), p. 55.

59 Ibid., p. 65.

60 Ibid., p. 69. Emphasis added.

61 Andrew Murray. "The Power of the Blood of Jesus." Date of retrieval: August 31, 2011 (http://www.worldinvisible.com/library / murray/5f00.0572/5f00.0572.08.htm).

62 Paul Brand and Phillip Yancey. *In His Image* (Grand Rapids, MI: Zondervan, 1984), p. 78.

63 Paul P. Enns promotes penal substitution and lists seven other "false theories": Ransom to Satan, Recapitulation, Commercial (Satisfaction), Moral Influence, Example, Governmental, and Accident (*The Moody Handbook of Theology* [Chicago, IL: Moody Press, 1989], Chapter 24). Enns, however, fails to mention *Christus Victor*, a popular theory since the early twentieth century. Oliver Crisp writes about McLeod Campbell's theory,

called nonpenal substitution (*International Journal of Systematic Theology*, "Non-Penal Substitution," October 2007). Further, editors James Beily and Paul Eddy (*The Nature of the Atonement* [Downers Grove, IL: InterVarsity Press, 2006]) write about two other theories, named "Healing" and "Kaleidoscope." The total is twelve, but there are others.

64 Paul Eddy and James Beilby (ed.). *The Nature of the Atonement.* "The Atonement: An Introduction" (Downers Grove, IL: InterVarsity Press, 2006), p. 11.

65 Richard A. Burridge. *Four Gospel, One Jesus?* (Grand Rapids, MI: Wm. B. Eerdmans Publishing, 2005), pp. 1–5. Second edition.

66 Although most evangelicals don't know it, this is called the penal substitution atonement theory. They just know it as *the* explanation for the sacrifice of Christ.

67 Greg A. Boyd. *The Nature of the Atonement.* "Christus Victor Response, Penal Substitution View." James Beilby and Paul Eddy (ed.), (Downers Grove, IL: InterVarsity Press, 2006), p. 104.

68 Philip Yancey. *What's So Amazing About Grace?* (Grand Rapids, MI: Zondervan Publishing House, 1997), p. 11.

Please visit
www.SeeingGodDifferently.com
to read more about God as Father,
join in on the disucssion, and order more books.
You can contact Eddie at Eddie@SeeingGodDifferently.com.